CUSTOMER'S ORDER NO.				DATE		

NAME *John + Janet Bollette*

ADDRESS *Craftsberg*

CITY, STATE, ZIP

SOLD BY	CASH	C.O.D.	CHARGE	ON ACCT.	MDSE. RETD.	PAID OUT

	QUAN.	DESCRIPTION	PRICE	AMOUNT
1	1	Book		25 —
2				1 75
3		25		
4		9		
5		175		26 75
6				
7				
8				
9				
10				
11				
12				

RECEIVED BY

February 2003

To John and Janet,
    May you enjoy traveling
with me and seeing the
flowers I discovered.

        Sincerely,
    Phyllis Joy Hammond

Traveling
with
Wildflowers
from Newfoundland to Alaska

Quechee Gorge State Park, Vermont
United States

Traveling
with
Wildflowers
from Newfoundland to Alaska

by

PHYLLIS JOY HAMMOND

ACKNOWLEDGEMENTS

I would like to thank the following for their help with my book: Gloria Pierre for her patience in editing my manuscript, and Alan Barrett and Judy Gibbs for additional help. For flower identification—Dr. R. R. Ogilvie, Curator of Botany, the Royal British Columbia Museum, Victoria, British Columbia, Verna E. Pratt, author of Alaskan wildflower guide books, Michael Burzynski, Interpreter, Gros Morne National Park, Newfoundland, Todd Boland, Botanist of the Memorial University Botanical Garden, St. John's, Newfoundland, Keith Dueholm for his identification of United States western flowers, and many others for their encouragement and practical advice.

ISBN 1-55056-626-1

P. J. Hammond
Box 3801, Lake Road
Newport Center, Vermont 05857

Book Design by Phyllis Joy Hammond
Design & Assembly by David Rankin Graphics, Cleveland, Ohio
Color Separations by Pop Color, Burlington, Vermont & David Rankin Graphics
Printed and bound by Friesens, Altona, Manitoba, Canada

This book is dedicated to Milton D. Hammond, my husband, for his willingness to try and stop at a moment's notice to let me view and sketch some wildflower and for his companionship as we drove the thousands of miles for the completion of this book.

Wood Lily

Sitka Burnett

CONTENTS

INTRODUCTION

We had stopped at The Memorial University Botanical Garden in St. John's to have the wildflowers I had been painting identified. I had returned to Newfoundland with my husband for the second time to paint its extraordinary landscape, only to find the weather cold, pack ice jamming the Gulf of St. Lawrence, fog hanging over everything, colors flat, and light uninteresting. To keep my trip from total disaster, I turned to the wildflowers that I discovered growing everywhere and blossoming profusely despite the cold.

By a series of extraordinary events we happened to meet Todd Boland, one of Newfoundland's fine wildflower botanists, in the parking lot. Standing outside, he identified all the plants in my pictures. But what was to prove even more important—evidently seeing something in my sketches—he encouraged me to continue painting the flowers of his province as we traveled back to Port aux Basques and the ferry. It was from this chance meeting and encouragement that my focus on painting wildflowers was to grow and our adventures with wildflowers start.

The more we traveled the more my interest in knowing the names of the plants I was seeing and my desire to share their beauty with others by painting them expanded. This interest led us to drive to Alaska three times, to Montana, back to Alberta, to Maine and to Newfoundland for a third visit—over 52,000 miles.

I was not a botanical painter. I had to discipline myself to study how leaves attached to stems, and to count leaflets (if there were one to eight pairs, it was one kind of vetch, if nine to eighteen, another). I would forget to take notes as to where the plant was growing, whether the stem was hairy or smooth and, oh yes, look at the bottom leaf. If it is the size of a plate it is a Schreber's aster! I discovered there are over 100 varieties of goldenrod growing in my state of Vermont alone; I knew two.

Wildflowers are a source of great amazement. To bike along a road you have lived on for thirty years and see six new wildflowers within the space of 100 feet, this is humbling. It is also disconcerting to suddenly find a plant that you had vainly sought for weeks throughout the West growing in your own pasture!

We all have a certain number of wildflowers that we readily recognize. Daisies are a good example. But I am discovering beyond daisies a whole host of daisy-like flowers: chamomiles, feverfews, fleabanes, and as you travel, the genus may stay the same but the species more often than not is different. The uniqueness, originality, variety, endless adaptations, and exquisite beauty of wildflowers inspires me.

A remarkable characteristic of wildflowers is their indifference to soil. No matter how gravelly, abused or discarded the soil may be, some wildflower will happily grow in it. I remember stopping our motor home to get water at a new gas station in Juneau, Alaska. Still scattered around were piles of rubbish and gravel. On one flowered a beautiful tall willow-herb. Another scene comes to mind. We were driving through the Pacific Northwest mourning the devastation created by the cut-and-burn practice of the loggers, when one such area was covered with a sea of fireweed and foxgloves. This sign of the earth's ability to renew itself truly lifts the spirits.

So much can be learned from wildflowers. It is cause for wonder that these natural beautifiers of the earth exist without human care. The fact that they flourish happily whether anyone sees them or not gives me much food for thought. But what moves me most is their exemplification of the phrase: "Blessed are the meek; for they shall inherit the earth."

Traveling with wildflowers enriches one's life and can make every trip more interesting. This book is designed to help travelers identify wildflowers as they stop at various areas of interest in the northern regions from Newfoundland to Alaska. It also aims to share with others the special qualities of loveliness that the artist saw in these flowers and the adventures arising from such encounters.

Honeysuckle

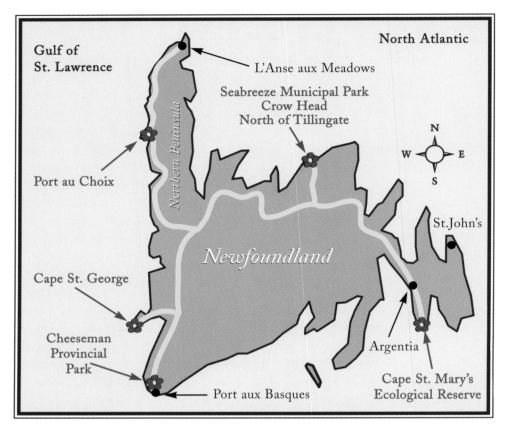

Gulf of St. Lawrence

North Atlantic

L'Anse aux Meadows

Seabreeze Municipal Park
Crow Head
North of Tillingate

Northern Peninsula

Port au Choix

Newfoundland

Cape St. George

St.John's

Cheeseman Provincial Park

Argentia

Cape St. Mary's Ecological Reserve

Port aux Basques

Chapter 1
THE BEGINNING
Newfoundland

J.T. CHEESEMAN PROVINCIAL PARK
Highway One, Trans-Canada Highway

CAPE ST. GEORGE
End of Highway 460

NORTHERN PENINSULA
Highway 430

SEABREEZE MUNICIPAL PARK
Crow Head, north of Twillingate, Highway 330

CAPE ST. MARY'S ECOLOGICAL RESERVE
Highway 100

Foreign Visitor

13

J.T. CHEESEMAN PROVINCIAL PARK
Highway One, Trans-Canada Highway

On arriving at Port aux Basques, Newfoundland, one is greeted by an extraordinary landscape—a land of flat mountains, bogs, dwarf trees, and very little tillable soil. Geologists believe that the movement of the great glaciers across the island scraped the top soil from the land and deposited it in the ocean, thus explaining the extraordinary richness of the fishing grounds southwest of the island.

If one is arriving at Port aux Basques by ferry in the evening or leaving early in the morning, Cheeseman Provincial Park is an excellent stop for campers because of its proximity to the ferry terminus. Named for a former head of the island's fisheries, its ample campsites, accommodations for large tour groups, and superb hiking trail joining the campgrounds to the beach make it a desirable spot to stay and explore. From its stony beach on a clear day, one can catch a glimpse of the great Cape Ray Lighthouse, which is a short drive from the park. Recently a small museum has opened adjacent to the lighthouse to exhibit some of the interesting artifacts being found by the archeologists digging in the area.

On our first visit to Newfoundland in late June, pack ice filled the Gulf of St. Lawrence making fishing impossible and the ferry to Labrador inoperative. In Cheeseman the leaves on the shrubs were just beginning to unfurl! Amelanchiers flowered everywhere. Here their common name is chuckley-pears. Lower to the ground marsh marigolds, rhodora, and Labrador tea bloomed. As we drove inland along Highway 1, we saw stunning masses of the purplish-rose rhodora growing much as fireweed does for miles along the Alaskan highways.

We discovered "Sea-witches" or witches' brooms in this park. These ball-like evergreen growths, caused by a fungus, appear on the tops of the stunted black spruce trees growing in the bogs. Some bogs have a great many; others, only a few; and some, none at all.

On a recent trip in mid-July (still another late growing season) I was invited to hike the long Smokey Cape Walking/Fitness Trail from the campsite to the beach with a park guide. She was a delight, for she knew not only the location but the names of unusual flowers. I cannot remember ever being greeted by such an array of flowers. It was a short walk; we never got beyond the woods. The lady's slippers, in shades of pink to deepest red, were breathtaking. The white fringed orchis and dragon's mouth were pointed out. Pitcher plants nodded in the gentle wind; the varying shades of their insect-trapping leaves were fascinating.

1 Bog Laurel, *Kalmia polifolia*
2 Pink Lady's Slipper
   Cypripedium acaule
3 Twinflower, *Linnaea borealis*

4 Starflower, *Trientalis borealis*
5 Dragon's Mouth, *Arethusa bulbosa*
6 White Fringed Orchis
   Habenaria blephariglottis

7 Pitcher Plant, *Sarracenia purpurea*

Twinflowers congregated in great colonies filling the ground with pale pink bells. There were still traces of blooming Labrador tea.

To sit on the boardwalk in the warm sunshine surrounded by more flowers than one could possibly paint is a privilege for any flower painter. My two days in this park were not enough; all of Newfoundland beckoned.

CAPE ST. GEORGE
End of Highway 460

Perhaps it was the combination of magnificent sunlight, azure-blue waters, marvelous patterns of a great surf breaking on the rocks below, and dramatic midday shadows but, whatever it was, our visit to Cape St. George was most memorable, its rugged beauty awesome. The discovery of extraordinary wildflowers, dwarfed by the constant exposure to the winds, only added to the wonder of this location.

When we first visited the Cape, it seemed undiscovered by tourists. The flowers grew undisturbed, with only one or two small trails

Cape St. George

Golden Ragwort
Senecio aureus

Willow
Salix uva-ursi

Capaea hortensis

Marsh Violet
Viola palustris

Tansy
Tanacetum huronense

Field Milkvetch
Oxytropis campestris

Hyssop-leaved Fleabane
Erigeron hyssopifolius

Harebell
*Campanula
rotundifolia*

through them and the small dirt road connecting the Cape to Highway 460. This was not the case on a later visit.

After exploring the dramatic rocks, I turned my gaze to the plants, only to realize that I could identify just a violet and a small two-inch willow. There was a plethora of plants among the mosses, none more than three or four inches high, all exquisitely formed. At the time I did not know that I was seeing field milkvetch, dwarf golden ragwort, hyssop-leaved fleabane, and tansy, a tiny yellow flower with minute circular petals and amazingly ornate leaves. The only tansy I knew was two to four feet tall and very rank. The small snail *Cepaea hortensis* was discovered, not at the water's edge but high up on the cliff's edge eating a dandelion leaf. This genus shares the general distinction that slugs have in the United States, that of unwanted mollusk pests.

While the flora along the coastal regions are distinctive, the ones found at Cape St. George seemed more extraordinary than elsewhere. And never have I seen a more dramatic cape.

NORTHERN PENINSULA
Highway 430

For unparalleled beauty one should not miss the drive up Newfoundland's Northern Peninsula. On one side of the road is the startling brilliance of the vast blue Gulf of St. Lawrence; on the other, the great, flat Long Range Mountains rising in the distance, and in the foreground, bogs of every shape and size. If the sun is shining, one's neck is constantly swiveling from one side to another, so enthralling is every view. For flower lovers, each scenic turn-out becomes a place of discovery. Miniature flowers abound at every stop, especially on the ocean side.

From the parking lot of Western Brook Pond in grand Gros Morne National Park, one can hike inland to take an informative boat trip through a fjord. Walking over the bog on the raised wooden boardwalk at the beginning of the trail, one discovers the showy, leafy-white orchis or scent bottles, false Solomon's seal, leatherleaf, bog rosemary, chuckley pears, chocolate flower geums, iris, yellow rattle, fall meadow rue, and giant horsetails.

1 Buffaloberry, *Shepherdia canadensis*
2 *Dryas integrifolia* (in seed)
3 Daisy Fleabane, *Erigeron hyssopifolius*
4 Aaron's Rod, *Sedum rosea*
5 Harebell, *Campanula rotundifolia*
6 Grove Sandwort, *Moehringia lateriflora*
7 Partridgeberry
   Vaccinium vitis-idaea (fungus-infected)
8 Dwarf Arctic Willow, *Salix vestita*
9 Starry False Solomon's Seal
   Smilacina stellata
10 Pink Pyrola, *Pyrola asarifolia*

A few miles further north on the road one sees the fascinating rock formation on the ocean side known as The Arches. A stop here reveals an altogether different group of flowers. The charming bird's-eye primrose, as well as the six-inch coltsfoot with its yellow flower in seed (the same species common in the United States) can be seen. Green orchis, butterworts, harebells, and silverweeds—countless other flowers—fill the area between the rocks and the parking lot. Since this site is very popular with tourists, measures have been taken to protect the plants through use of signs and walkways.

Many stops later we arrived at Hawk's Bay to camp and hike the interesting flower-rich commemorative Hogan Trail. The next day we detoured to see the Archaic Indian site and Point Riche lighthouse at Port au Choix. From a distance one has no idea that the green area around the lighthouse is a carpet of wildflowers! For a flower lover, it was like finding treasure in a field. Exquisite smoothleaf mountain avens, heathers, mosses, alpine willows, pyrolas, tiny red and white saxifrages, minute yellow roseroots, and soapberries were found. Unfortunately, no effort has been made to protect the vegetation at this location, no paths established; it seems likely that this situation will change, as a new Visitors' Center is expected to open nearby.

Almost at the end of Highway 430, one finds the splendid Museum L'Anse aux Meadows, commemorating the only known Viking (or Norse) settlement in North America dating from the 11th century. Visiting this spot had a special significance for me because, when in Iceland, I stayed at a farmhouse adjacent to where Eric the Red had lived and near the beach from which he and his compatriots set sail for the West and Newfoundland's great Northern Peninsula. The name L'Anse aux Meadows is a corruption of the French name L'anse-aux-meduses meaning Jellyfish Cove.

It is from Highway 430 that one takes the ferry to Labrador, sees the raised gardens dug out of the peat bogs, and views many small fishing villages from which the fishermen go daily out to sea. It was while traveling this road that we gained new insights into the resoluteness and courage of the Newfoundland people.

The great Northern Peninsula tells the story not only of the ancient peoples who came here, but also of those who continue to struggle with sail and soil to make Newfoundland their home. The coastal beauty of the peninsula, bog ponds, glorious flowers, and Gros Morne National Park enchant and enrich all those who come this way.

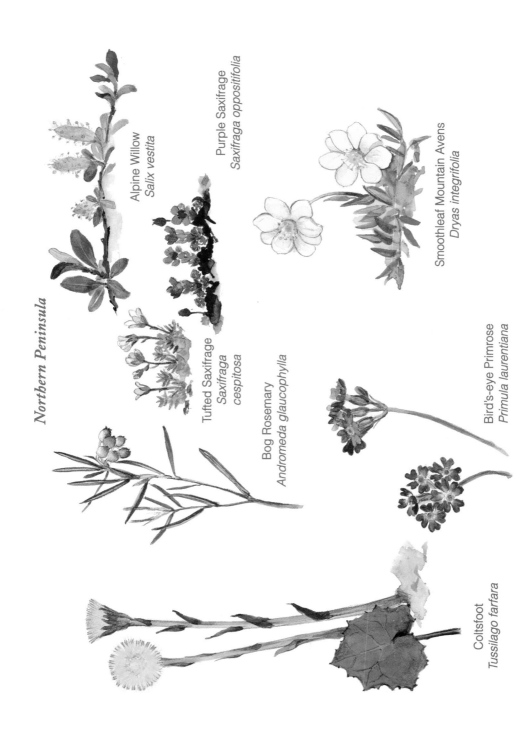

Northern Peninsula

Alpine Willow
Salix vestita

Purple Saxifrage
Saxifraga oppositifolia

Smoothleaf Mountain Avens
Dryas integrifolia

Tufted Saxifrage
Saxifraga cespitosa

Bog Rosemary
Andromeda glaucophylla

Bird's-eye Primrose
Primula laurentiana

Coltsfoot
Tussilago farfara

21

No one should miss this scenic municipal park a few miles north of Twillingate on the north Atlantic Ocean. It is to these waters that the great icebergs of the Arctic drift. Long before reaching Twillingate, one begins to see them dotting the bays and coves. On both of our visits to this park, these spectacular northern giants were aground in the bay in front of the campground. Beside them, a passing weather helicopter looked like a fly. We could hear their dissolving chunks of ice clinking like ice cubes in a glass as they floated onto the stony beach below.

Twillingate has a rich fishing history and an outstanding museum. On the dock, we traded Vermont maple syrup for monstrous crabs; at our campsite we shared our bounty with the campers next to us.

As we hiked the park and adjacent land, we saw large colonies of starry false Solomon's seal, dwarf coastal iris no higher than three inches, blooming exquisitely, and crowberry, juniper, and mosses of all colors. The

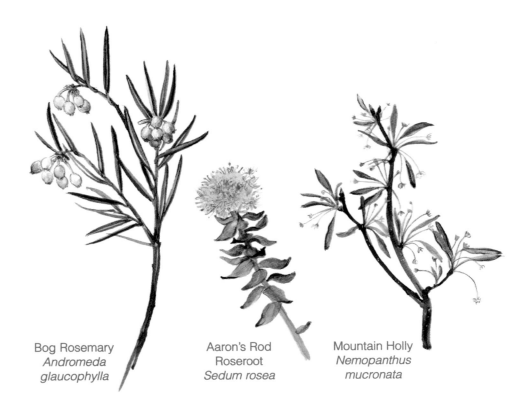

Bog Rosemary
Andromeda glaucophylla

Aaron's Rod
Roseroot
Sedum rosea

Mountain Holly
Nemopanthus mucronata

1 Lady's Mantle
  Alchenilla sp.
2 Northern Goldenrod
  Solidago multiradiata
3 Butterwort
  Pinguicula vulgaris
4 Curled Dock, *Rumex crispus*

5 Dwarf Coastal Iris
  Iris setosa or hookeri
6 Yarrow, *Achillea
  millefolium (Forma borealis)*
7 Seaside Plaintain, *Plantago maritima*
8 Oysterleaf or Sea Mertensia
  Mertensia maritima

nearby great red lighthouse with its foot-thick walls had yellow roseroot growing close to its base. I was familiar with the pink variety. One also finds dwarf northern goldenrod, *Solidago multiradiata*, common in similar climates across the continent. The small museum and gift shop serving tea add a new grace note to lighthouse visits.

Another plant new to me in this area was the delicate mountain holly, a shrub common throughout Newfoundland. On the beach, one discovers oysterleaf and seaside plantain. Because the season was so backward on our second trip—almost a month late—many wildflowers were seen blooming which would normally have gone to seed by the beginning of July.

Throughout the park one sees old mining equipment from the once-active mine on the nearby promontory. There are also odd hollows built into the ground, which are said to be the early settlers' old root cellars. One is drawn to return again and again to this small, rugged coastal park, to wonder at its extraordinary icebergs and to enjoy the many flowers tucked in among the rocks.

CAPE ST. MARY'S ECOLOGICAL RESERVE
Highway 100

Cape St. Mary's Ecological Reserve is located on a tip of the Avalon Peninsula approximately 126 miles, or 200 kilometers, south of St. John's, the capital of Newfoundland. It is one of five reserves established to protect this province's seabird breeding population; here one finds the third largest gannetry in North America. Besides adult gannets, the air is alive with flying black-legged kittiwakes, razorbills, common and thick-billed mures, various gulls, and black guillemots. Located 400 feet above the ocean with great cliffs falling directly to the water below, this reserve is a spectacular place to visit. The marvel of this spot for persons accustomed to only occasional backyard birds and migrating crows and geese can easily be imagined.

Once the gannet eggs hatch, thousands of down-covered nestlings whiten the cliffs like an early season blizzard. They can also be seen at eye level in great numbers on a towering sea-stack known as Bird Rock, about 120 feet away from a shore viewing area. How the adult birds find their own young in such a high density nesting site fills one with wonder. Young gannets, unlike other birds, do not leave their nests until fall migration, so anyone who comes to this reserve in the summer can enjoy

1 Common Speedwell
   Veronica officinalis
2 Three-Toothed Cinquefoil
   Potentilla tridentata
3 Marsh Violet, *Viola palustris*
4 Moss Campion, *Silene acaulis*

5 Tawny Cotton-Grass
   Eriophorum virginicum
6 Buckbean, *Menyanthes trifoliata*
7 Cotton-Grass, *Eriophorum spissum*
8 Cotton-Grass
   Eriophorum angustifolium

Bird Rock

this spectacle. Seabirds in such numbers and varieties and so close are a new experience to almost everyone who comes to this location.

This area is also filled with wildflowers. As one starts the drive into the Reserve from the main road, there is a swampy area filled with flowering buckbean. Their trifoliate leaves reach up out of the still water, and their fuzzy white-bearded flowers beautify every pool in which they grow. These water-loving plants can be seen throughout the province. Pitcher plants dot both sides of the road. Cotton-grass grows freely; these sedges flourish around the world in the northern regions. One can see two kinds of white, as well as the rarer tawny variety, here. Bush honey-suckle grows among the shrubs lining the road; the ditches alongside sparkle with the pink hue of sundews. Close to the lighthouse, one finds violets and dainty, tiny moss campion in clusters of all sizes.

The wind was fierce as we hiked the 30-minute trail out to the observation point to see the birds. Whenever the land dipped below the wind line, plants flourished two to three feet high. The cold prevented my lingering for a look at the flowers; but on a later visit I saw iris, both tall and dwarf, blooming profusely along the trail and white three-toothed

Cliffs of St. Mary's

cinquefoil dancing in the wind. Cinnamon ferns and asters were seen in the more sheltered spots.

In 1995, a new modern Interpretive Center was completed replacing the small one in the old lighthouse. It is designed to give the thousands of summer visitors a fuller appreciation of this reserve and the shore birds that inhabit its cliffs.

The drive down to Cape St. Mary's, with its sweeping coastal views, makes a grand daytrip for those waiting to take the night ferry from Argentia back to North Sydney, Nova Scotia. The trip can be broken with a stop at Castle Hill National Historic Park, where the fort takes one back to perhaps the earliest permanent settlement of Newfoundland. It is also possible to continue the drive around the Avalon Peninsula beyond Cape St. Mary's to still another region of this wonderful island.

Baked-apple Berry or Cloudberry

Rubus chamaemorus

ESQUA BOG
Hartand Hill Road, Woodstock, Vermont

SMUGGLER'S NOTCH STATE PARK
Mountain Road, Stowe, Vermont

JACQUES CARTIER STATE PARK
Route 12, St Lawrence Seaway, New York

THEODORE ROOSEVELT NATIONAL PARK
South Unit
Buffalo Gap Campground
I-94, North Dakota

PACIFIC BEACH FLOWERS
Route 101, California/Oregon

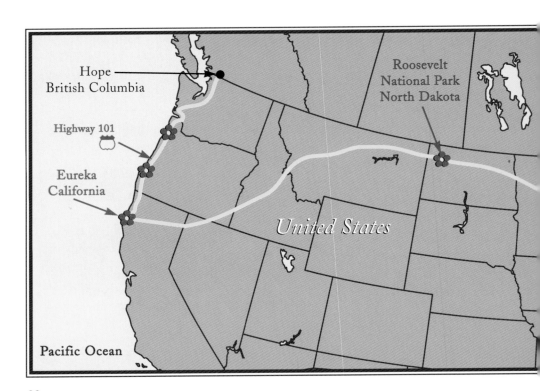

CHAPTER 2
WESTWARD BOUND
Northern United States
Spring

WEST QUODDY HEAD STATE PARK
Lubec, Maine

BAXTER STATE PARK
Route 11, Millinocket, Maine

WHITE MOUNTAIN NATIONAL FOREST
I-93 and Route 112, New Hampshire

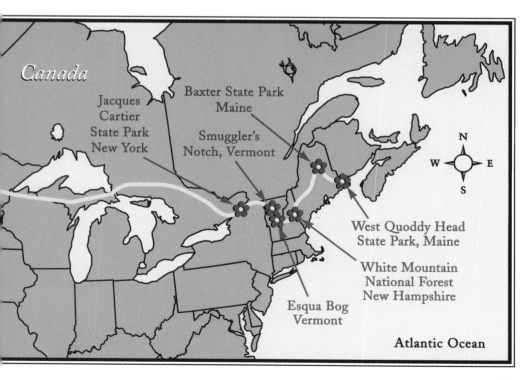

WEST QUODDY HEAD STATE PARK
Lubec, Maine

The West Quoddy Head lighthouse with its red and white candy stripes is a dominant landmark in this park marking the most easterly point of land on the United States coastline. This day-use park offers some of the finest and most spectacular hiking found on the Maine coast. The great perpendicular cliffs, 24-to-28 foot tides, ruggedness of terrain, and excellent trails make it an area one wants to return to again and again.

In mid-June one should hike out to High Point to see the great clumps of blue flag iris, which are so unexpected in this windswept, exposed spot. The flowers and unfolding beauty of the coastal cliffs make continuing on to Green Point at the end of the park a most rewarding experience. For many this long hike may seem too arduous; if so, there is a shorter trail that crosses over into Quoddy's memorable interior bog. It is a gem! The interpretation markers are excellent for both flower identification and information about bog evolution. Starting on the boardwalk, one sees the extraordinary variety of colors that sphagnum moss gives to bogs. The shades range from deepest red to orange, pink and spring greens. And over the moss the dainty tiny-threaded leaves of the small cranberry wander. Sundews grow in such profusion here that they turn the earth a sparkling rose. These and the burgundy pitcher plants are excellent examples of the insect-eating wildflowers found in this area. The latter bloom in July.

After the rigors of the ocean trail, returning to the parking area on the interior level path can be a welcome contrast. With the glorious ocean views left behind, one's eyes are drawn to the wealth of very small plants on either side of this spruce-covered lane. Studying the small glossy-leaved mountain cranberries, paired blooms of the dainty twin flowers, delicate starflowers, and mosses along the way makes one realize anew the significance of nature's smallest gifts.

The resonance of the foghorn, the crashing of the waves, the occasional appearance of whales, the quiet coves, the grandeur of the cliffs, the world of wildflowers, all enrich every visitor who steps onto these grounds. The park gives to each a suitcase full of treasured recollections.

Round-leafed Sundew, *Drosera rotundifolia*

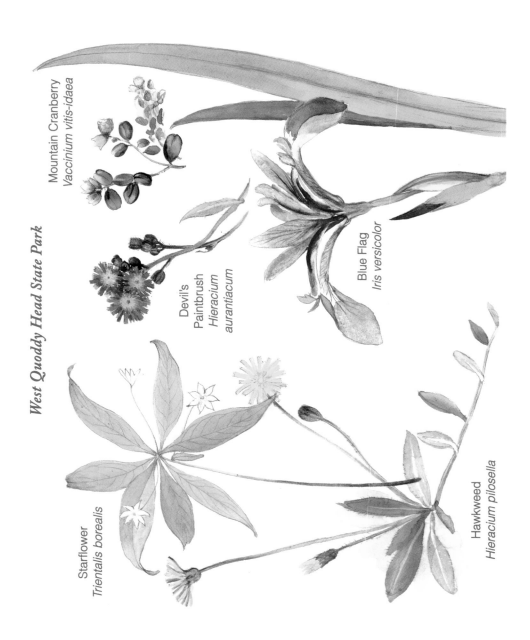

West Quoddy Head State Park

Mountain Cranberry
Vaccinium vitis-idaea

Devil's
Paintbrush
*Hieracium
aurantiacum*

Blue Flag
Iris versicolor

Starflower
Trientalis borealis

Hawkweed
Hieracium pilosella

BAXTER STATE PARK
Route 11, Millinocket, Maine

There is in the middle of northern Maine an extraordinary wilderness area of 202,064 acres known as Baxter State Park. In this park is found Mt. Katahdin, the most northerly point of the Appalachian Trail. This public footpath stretches 2,155 miles along the spine of the Appalachian Mountains from Maine to Georgia and challenges all who venture on it. Baxter State Park provides a fitting environment for this trail. Rugged outdoor people flock to this spot to test their endurance and survival skills. I met a couple from the Midwest who were just starting on the trail to hike to Georgia six months away. They had sold their home, left their jobs and told their 22-year-old son he must now live on his own. My reason for coming here was to paint wildflowers and to see if I could enjoy myself in such a wilderness setting.

Baxter has none of the soft park amenities most of us are used to—running water, flush toilets, paved roads. No motor homes are permitted. Tent and lean-to camping are the rule. Its few dirt roads are narrow and washboardy. Firearms are forbidden as are pets, no aircraft can ever land there, and the only roads permitted within its borders are those to the campsites. Percival P. Baxter, a former governor of Maine, set aside this land as a park for the people of Maine and a sanctuary for all wildlife within its borders.

I was not disappointed in my decision to visit this park. Although the first wave of spring flowers had passed, early July found the rare white lady's slipper blooming near my campsite. Around Daicey Pond paintbrush and meadow rue were observed just starting to bloom; Labrador tea and sheep laurel were abundant in the damp location of the pond. One of the sights I loved best was the colonies of common wood sorrel with their gentle flowers clustered among the roots of the great spruce and fir trees. I discovered the new pink growth of the checkerberry and noticed that occasionally the plants still retained their fruit amid last year's evergreen leaves.

Weather prevented a lengthy stay at Baxter, but there is much more to see. I plan to return, better equipped for camping at this level.

1 Ragged Robin, *Lychnis flos-cuculi*
2 White Moccasin Flower
   Cypripedium acaule
3 Sheep Laurel, *Kalmia angustifolia*
4 Wild Sarsaparilla, *Aralia nudicaulis*
5 Labrador Tea, *Ledum groenlandicum*

6 Leatherleaf
   Chamaedaphne calyculata
7 Birdfoot Trefoil, *Lotus corniculatus*
8 Wintergreen or Checkerberry
   Gaultheria procumbens
9 Common Wood Sorrel, *Oxalis montana*

The New Hampshire White Mountain National Forest is one of the most loved and scenically beautiful areas of Northeastern America. It includes the Franconia Notch State Park where the Old Man of the Mountain can be viewed. The sight of the great rock profile jutting out from cliffs 1200 feet above the road has inspired thousands since its discovery by white men in the early 1800s. Long before that time it was revered by the region's Indians. Casual visitors and outdoor enthusiasts flock to this park to hike and bike its splendid tarred paths, climb the mountains, swim, fish a little, relax, gain inspiration, see the flume, visit the basin, and gaze at the gorge. Trail heads are almost always filled with cars. The Appalachian trail crosses its boundaries.

The National Forest also includes the Kancamagus Highway, a scenic two-lane drive going east and west between Lincoln and Conway. It is one of New England's most glorious roads for fall foliage viewing. Along its sides one finds campgrounds and trails adapted to the less athletically inclined. We enjoy both spots when we visit New Hampshire. All the roads through this region offer great vistas of beauty and rural settings.

My flowers are not from any one specific area in the National Forest. The rhodora was from a field we chanced to pass. I had not seen such a display of this plant since Newfoundland. Jack-in-the pulpit and yellow clintonia abound in the spring woods, yellow goat's beard in the open spots. Not pictured is the hobblebush. This shrub, growing above the wildflowers, has large white flower clusters which brighten the dark woods wherever it blooms. Its opposite plate-like leaves and red/black fruit make it easily recognizable. The area around the Flume Visitors' Center of Franconia Notch offers a good opportunity for wildflower viewing. Perhaps spring is the best time to look for wildflowers in the forest; the heavy foliage has not fully darkened the forest floor. But each season brings a steady progression of interesting flowers.

The casual sightseer, stopping to walk to Profile Lake for a superb view of the Old Man of the Mountain, or just driving through the Notch, cannot help being moved by the grandeur of this national treasure.

1 Rhodora
  Rhododendron canadense
2 Corn-Lily, *Clintonia borealis*
3 Lesser Daisy Fleabane
  Erigeron strigosus

4 Wild Lily-of-the-Valley
  Maianthemum canadense
5 Common Cinquefoil, *Potentilla simplex*
6 Bird's-Eye Speedwell
  Veronica chamaedrys

ESQUA BOG
Hartand Road, Woodstock, Vermont

Woodstock is one of the most delightful towns in all Vermont—the rural setting, charming Main Street with its many unique shops, the Vermont Institute of Natural Science's raptor center, and the educational Billings farm, all make it a centerpiece for many visitors to this state. It is certainly one of the most popular spots for fall foliage enthusiasts. As the mountains turn orange and red, the roads of this region become clogged with what the natives call "leaf peepers."

We have loved this area for a long time, always making trips to the nearby Quechee State Park for overnight camping. One always seems able to discover some new wildflower in the park or along the trails of nearby Quechee Gorge. The 165-foot gorge attracts thousands in the summer to photograph and wonder at this unique Vermont ice-age formation.

Generally one learns of nearby Esqua Bog, a 40-acre sanctuary just east of Woodstock, from wildflower enthusiasts. Owned and managed jointly by the New England Wildflower Society and Nature Conservancy, this preserve is the habitat of rare and diverse plants. It has both bog and woodland areas, and is the home of the endangered yellow lady slipper.

One clear fresh spring day, I quickly located the lady slippers, settled myself on the bog boardwalk, and started to paint. Looking around, I could also see long stemmed violets, marsh marigolds, star flowers, purple geums, blueberries, and foam flowers. Moisture-loving tamarack trees, ladened with new cones, dotted the area; blue flags were just beginning to open. It was a magical morning.

Those unfamiliar with bog plants will be delighted to find many in this sanctuary labeled with both common and botanical names. On leaving the boardwalk, the trail enters the wooded area, which can easily be traveled within an hour. The guest book at the entrance to the preserve reveals the extent of attraction this secluded site has for wildflower lovers and naturalists.

1 Slender Blue Flag, *Iris prismatica*
2 Smaller Yellow Lady Slipper
   Cypripedium paviflorum
3 Golden Alexanders, *Zizia aurea*

4 Dwarf Blueberry, *Vaccinium augustifolium*
5 Marsh Violet, *Viola cucullata*
6 Ground Pine or Club Moss, *Lycopodium Sp.*
7 Tamarack, *Larix laricina*

SMUGGLER'S NOTCH STATE PARK
Mountain Road, Stowe, Vermont

The Event of a Moment

Smuggler's Notch received its name during the period when President Thomas Jefferson passed an embargo forbidding American trade with Great Britain and Canada. This Act of 1807 caused severe hardships for northern Vermonters. Their natural markets were with nearby Canada, especially the city of Montreal. Many people, their livelihoods endangered, ignored the decree and continued to herd their cattle northward and carry goods back through the 1000-foot mountain notch leading towards Canada. Today there is a small state park encompassing this area, Smuggler's Notch State Park.

Having finished my painting on a day of extraordinary beauty, air soft, the sunlight shafting down to the forest floor in scintillating patterns, I saw a trillium of such magnificence and size that I could not believe my eyes. I drew closer to study it, puzzled that it did not quite conform to the trillium pattern I knew. Gradually it dawned on me that there was a triangular pattern of leaf stems below the soaring red fruit. The great leaves were stemmed! They were not attached directly to the plant. It seemed so right that such grandeur should have uniqueness as well. I determined to paint it.

The next morning I returned to the area. Imagine my consternation when I had trouble finding my specimen plant! Finally I recognized it, one leaf drooping and stained as if by a bird, and glistening fruit gone. Although the specialness was a bit marred, I painted it anyway.

Work finished, I decided to confirm the rarity of my trillium by comparing it with its other three-leafed neighbors. As I examined one of the plants, I noticed a red fruit directly under it. On lifting my gaze, I discovered the forest floor dotted with red jewels, either directly below the plants or rolled a few inches away. They were not on the ground yesterday. When had this happened? At night? What brought about this unified action throughout the woods? Did anyone hear the thud of the small fruit as they fell to the ground? It was the event of a moment and my trillium, in another part of the woods, was a part of this happening. I sensed a gracious governance at work as I stood there. It filled my thought with wonder and continues to do so every time I consider this moment. (I have since learned that possibly the plant was a painted trillium.)

JACQUES CARTIER STATE PARK
Route 12, St. Lawrence Seaway, New York

From northern Vermont Jacques Cartier State Park is a natural first stop on one's westward journeys. It is not the only park on the St. Lawrence Seaway, but it is the only one that boasts thousands of spring-blooming white trillium. If one's timing is correct, they spangle the roadsides as one drives into the campsites. But before reaching Jacques Cartier, one should see the marvelous Frederick Remington Museum in nearby Ogdensburg, New York. The impact and power of this artist's work can be experienced to no greater degree than in this museum, originally one of his homes. The western bronzes excite the imagination beyond words.

As one drives through the Jacques Cartier Park entrance in spring, the forest floor is spangled white. Overhead the delicate green of the hardwoods' new growth scarcely casts a shadow. The sunlight streams uninterruptedly to the ground. Trillium bursts forth in all sizes—from great white ones to the very small. Occasionally a flash of pink can be seen, a color that supposedly comes with age, but here the pink are just as fresh as any other bloom. All provide a breathtaking experience.

The St. Lawrence River laps at the shore down by the common area. There one can find a gentle columbine tucked away in a lee. As one walks back up the hill at the edge of the woods, cuckoo flower and barren strawberry can be seen. A rudimentary road into the woods reveals even more flowers blossoming. Violets and red trilliums are especially lovely. After a few weeks of spring, these flowers are replaced by jack-in-the-pulpits, waterleaves, three kinds of buttercups, and herb Roberts. At whatever time one comes to this gracious park during the growing season, there are be flowers to be discovered and enjoyed.

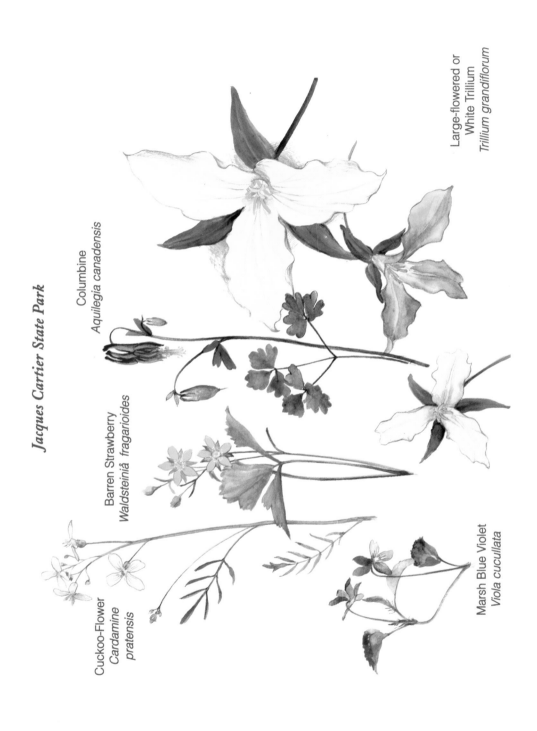

Jacques Cartier State Park

Columbine
Aquilegia canadensis

Large-flowered or
White Trillium
Trillium grandiflorum

Barren Strawberry
Waldsteinia fragarioides

Cuckoo-Flower
Cardamine pratensis

Marsh Blue Violet
Viola cucullata

Jacques Cartier State Park

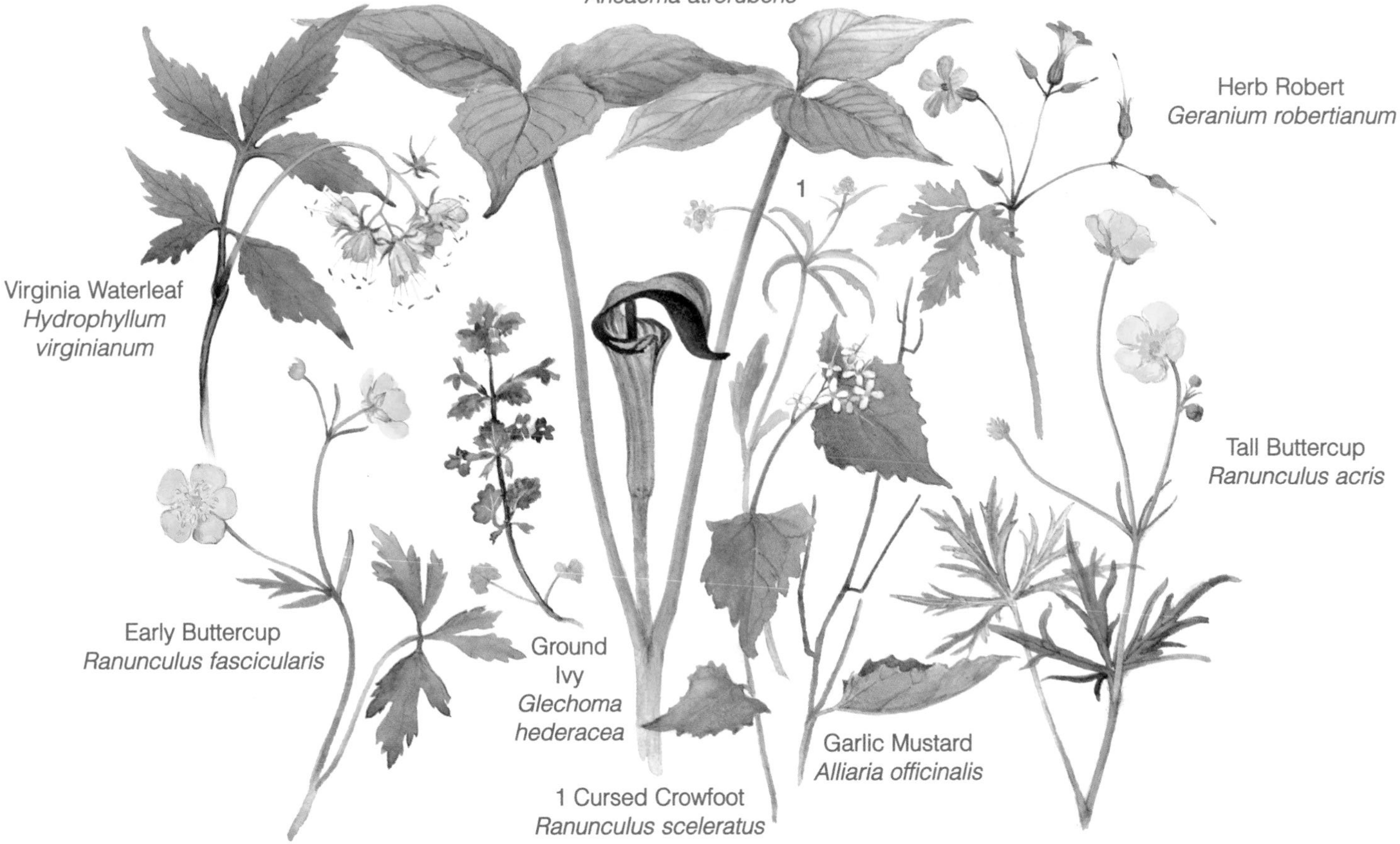

Herb Robert
Geranium robertianum

Tall Buttercup
Ranunculus acris

Garlic Mustard
Alliaria officinalis

Jack-in-the-pulpit
Arisaema atrorubens

1

Ground
Ivy
*Glechoma
hederacea*

1 Cursed Crowfoot
Ranunculus sceleratus

Virginia Waterleaf
*Hydrophyllum
virginianum*

Early Buttercup
Ranunculus fascicularis

Almost everyone who travels west or east on Route I-94 through North Dakota makes the short detour into Roosevelt National Park, which lies just this side of the Montana border. It is an area loved and made famous by President Theodore Roosevelt, and is now a glorious national park protecting the extraordinary beauty of the badlands for all mankind.

Standing on the high grassy rim outside the visitors' center, one sees below a panorama of the amazing landscape designated the Little Missouri River Badlands. Originally they were the bed of an inland sea. It is believed that the area began to form about 600,000 years ago when, through a chain of events, a glacier stopped the flow of the river northward and sent it instead flowing rapidly towards the east. The fast erosive action of the river combined with centuries of wind and weather gradually shaped the badlands into what we see today—a fantasia of layered shapes of shale, volcanic ash, clay, silt, sandstone, and coal made colorful by minerals deposited by the water. It is an awe-inspiring area, either hated or loved, according to one's point of view. We have visited this spot on every trip west and have hiked down to the valley floor for a closer look at the myriad patterns of eroded shapes and to study the vegetation.

We have stayed in the park's campsite in Medora, but our great love is the charming Buffalo Gap Campground just a little further on. It is a small microcosm of the badlands, intimate and friendly, in contrast with the overwhelming vastness of its neighbor. It has a small mountain (hill) that one can climb on a circular path for a view of the nearby colored layered landscape. At the top are interpretive signs explaining how and when the badlands were formed. The wildflowers on this little trail are delightful, and on the summit we once found evening stars blooming.

Around campsites and adjacent fields, wildflowers are abundant and extraordinary. Becoming acquainted with their names takes time for an Easterner because they are so unusual. We have visited this park both in spring and in August. The extravagant variety of spring flowers is thrilling, but the beauty of the rigid goldenrods, with their dense pure yellow ray flowers standing so upright on their sturdy stalks, makes an August visit equally rewarding. The rigid goldenrod is certainly one of the most gorgeous species in this family. Different varieties of thistle also abound in August as does leafy spurge. The latter plant is a fast growing weed introduction, a scourge to grain and native wildflowers of the region.

Buffalo Gap Campground

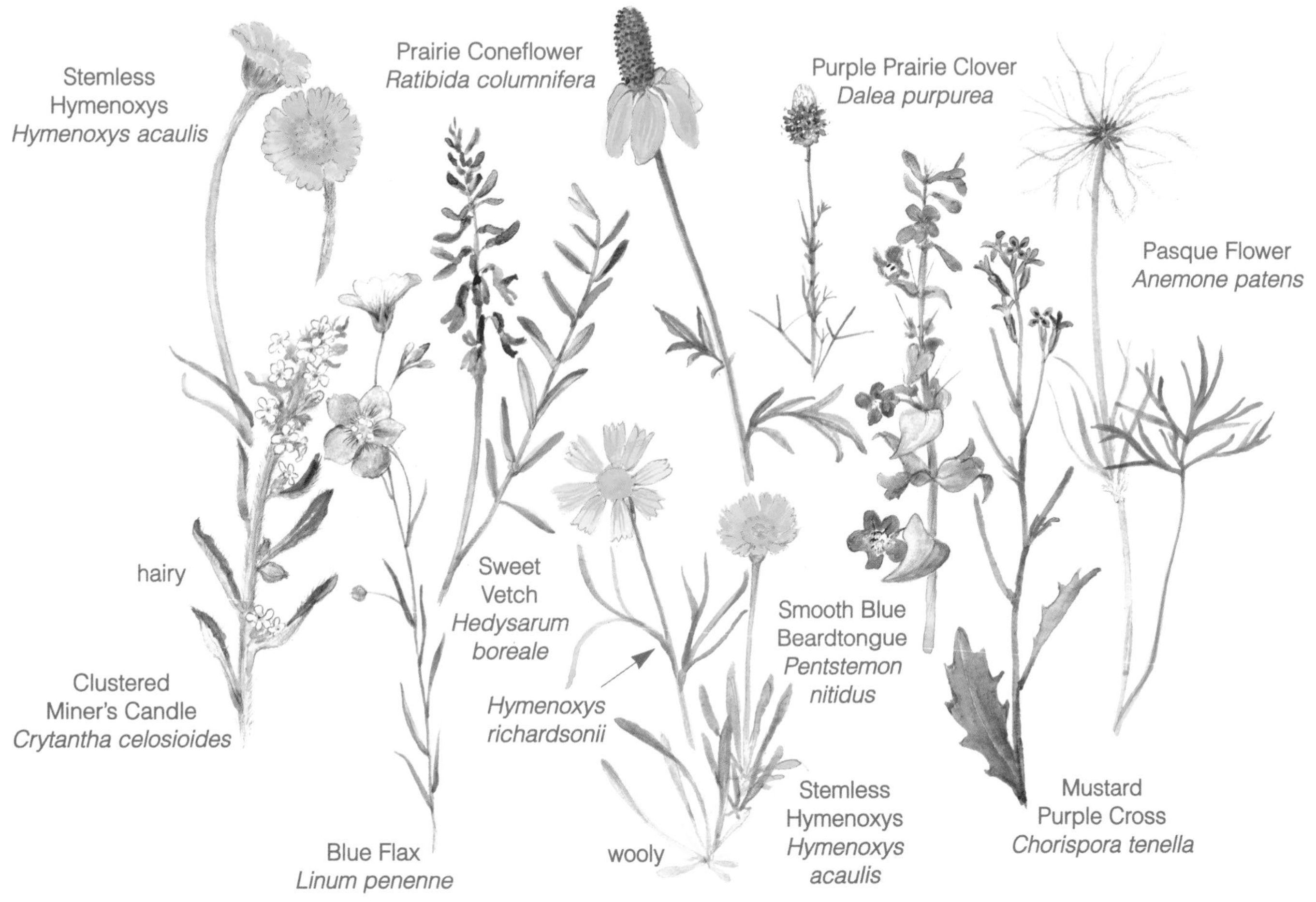

Pasque Flower
Anemone patens

Mustard
Purple Cross
Chorispora tenella

Purple Prairie Clover
Dalea purpurea

Smooth Blue
Beardtongue
*Pentstemon
nitidus*

Stemless
Hymenoxys
*Hymenoxys
acaulis*

wooly

Prairie Coneflower
Ratibida columnifera

Sweet
Vetch
*Hedysarum
boreale*

*Hymenoxys
richardsonii*

Blue Flax
Linum penenne

Stemless
Hymenoxys
Hymenoxys acaulis

hairy

Clustered
Miner's Candle
Crytantha celosioides

43

P.J.HAMMOND '98

PACIFIC BEACH FLOWERS
Route 101, California/Oregon

As we gained Route 101 from Route 20 in northern California, we had our first real meeting with beach flowers at Buena Vista Park, which is south of the famous Samoa House restaurant across the bridge from Eureka. For people who have always lived inland, seeing these flowers is a wonderful experience. They grow in such inhospitable conditions— sand, salt spray, wind—yet they flourish vigorously.

Buena Vista Park is on a bay shore of the Pacific Ocean, and the stunning yellow ice plant grows on its dunes. These extraordinary multi-petaled flowers, with their fat, triangular, succulent leaves and stems, spread in low masses over the sand. The structure of these plants permits storing moisture from ocean spray and fogs.

As one drives northward along the coast, the panorama of beaches invites the traveler to explore. As one does so, more flowers are discovered. The Pacific silverweed with its red runners and beach pea sprawl everywhere on the sand. They are often seen intermingling with the northern dune tansy and yellow verbena. The yellow verbena is another example of a coastal plant with succulent leaves. Silver-top, with its unusual flowers, is also present. Beach plants sometimes have hairs on their stems for moisture retention as do some desert flowers. The dune flowers also have extensive root systems that anchor them in the sands around them as well as increase their ability to gather and store water.

Nature seems to want to cover the earth with loveliness, and wildflowers are certainly one of its tools for achieving this. Not even the forbidding Pacific coastal environment has been able to prevent wildflowers from growing in abundance. Scarcely a spot exists along these coastal waters where there is not some plant flourishing and spreading. Much can be learned from their example of adaptability and tenacity.

Waters of the Pacific - page 42-43

Pacific Beach Flowers

Yellow Ice Plant
Mesembryanthemum edule

Pacific Silverweed
Potentilla pacifica

Northern Dune Tansy
Tanacetum douglasii

Yellow Sand Verbena
Abronia latifolia

Beach Silvertop
Glehnia leiocarpa

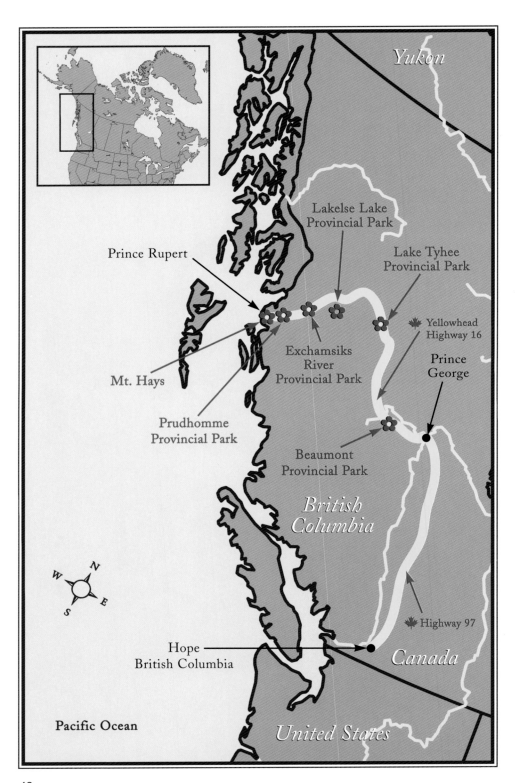

Yukon

Lakelse Lake
Provincial Park

Lake Tyhee
Provincial Park

Prince Rupert

Yellowhead
Highway 16

Prince
George

Mt. Hays

Exchamsiks
River
Provincial Park

Prudhomme
Provincial Park

Beaumont
Provincial Park

British
Columbia

Highway 97

Hope
British Columbia

Canada

Pacific Ocean

United States

BEAUMONT PROVINCIAL PARK

TYHEE PROVINCIAL PARK

LAKELSE LAKE PROVINCIAL PARK

EXCHAMSIKS RIVER PROVINCIAL PARK

PRUDHOMME PROVINCIAL PARK

HAYS MOUNTAIN BOG
Prince Rupert

Road to Prince Rupert, B.C.

Road to Prince Rupert

BEAUMONT PROVINCIAL PARK
Yellowhead Highway

The Canadian provinces' ability to create superb provincial parks is nowhere illustrated more clearly than on the Yellowhead Highway between Prince George and Prince Rupert, British Columbia. This 456-mile stretch of road is certainly one of the most scenic and park-filled regions in all of Canada. Here nature, in the form of some of the greatest peaks of the Canadian Rockies, green glacier-fed rivers, old growth forests, lakes and a fjord, conspires to make one of the most beautiful areas seen on the entire journey. It was an unexpected pleasure because there had been fog to the road level on our first trip four years earlier, and we had been completely ignorant of the magnificence we had missed.

As we left Prince George on our second trip to Alaska, we found ourselves with seven days to drive less than 500 miles. My husband's concern over our Prince Rupert ferry date had kept us at a very steady pace since our departure from Vermont. Because we had covered 3,550 miles in 17 days, we now had time to leisurely experience the parks that lay before us.

Our first stop was at Beaumont Provincial Park on Fraser Lake. This whole region rings with the name of Simon Fraser, explorer in the early 1800s. In addition to camping sites, both in woods and open areas, the park has a superb beach. Paved roads make biking a pleasure. As it was early in the season, we had the park almost entirely to ourselves. Spring flowers were blooming in great profusion everywhere. The forester told us where to find the park's outstanding blue clematis. I had all my flower books open trying to identify the plants I was seeing and painting. I recognized the black twinberry as some sort of honeysuckle, but the fairybell, showy Jacob's-ladder and tiny male flowers of the meadow-rue were a mystery to me at the time.

The following day found us stopping in Burns Lake to shop and refuel. About ten miles west of this town, the Canadian Rockies begin to appear.

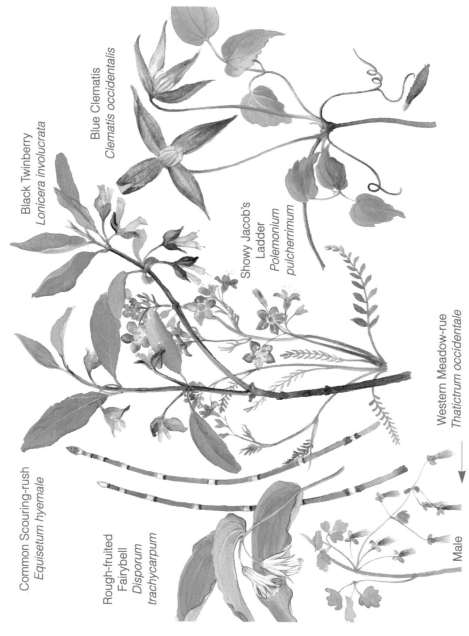

Beaumont Provincial Park

Black Twinberry
Lonicera involucrata

Blue Clematis
Clematis occidentalis

Showy Jacob's
Ladder
*Polemonium
pulcherrimum*

Common Scouring-rush
Equisetum hyemale

Rough-fruited
Fairybell
*Disporum
trachycarpum*

Western Meadow-rue
Thalictrum occidentale

Male

Smithers, B.C.

After Smithers, B.C.

Our next camping choice was Tyhee Provincial Park. This is a park one must not miss, if only to pause on top of the steep hill that leads down to the camping area. The view is staggering. One is encircled by the flow of mountain range after mountain range, all demanding to be seen at once. Both the evening and morning of our visit, sunlight shown on the mountains, and the air was so crystal clear that it was almost tangible. One never quite recovers from such a sight. My attempt to paint from here in the morning was feeble indeed; nature's art was so magnificent.

In the afternoon we left for Lakelse Lake Provincial Park, where we had had only an overnight stay on our first trip to Alaska. This visit was a revelation. Now we saw mountains and a grand old-growth forest soaring above us to great heights where previously we had seen only fog. The air was so still that every detail of the mountains could be seen twice: once as they were and a second time, reflected in the lake. I cannot imagine a place more suited to this artist and her woodsman husband. He photographed, measured, and celebrated the giant Sitka spruce and western cedar; (not far from here, he even found a small operating Alaskan mill with its chainsaw blade to watch). We hiked and biked the avenues of those awesome trees; it was a spiritual experience to be in their presence.

We lingered in this spot for four days. I had a chance to catch up on my work. The flowers were a marvel in the filtered sunlight. One saw bunchberry that, in their exuberance, climbed up and flowered on the trunk of a Sitka spruce. Clintonia dotted the woods and the cascading thimbleberry could be seen behind each campsite. Devil's club, which would follow us into Alaska, began to appear.

A word about devil's club, *Echinopanax horridum*. This huge plant, growing to eight feet, is most pervasive in the deep, moist woodland glades of the Inside Passage. One is likely to find devil's club where sunlight sifts through the dense overhead foliage of rainforests. Their foot-sized leaves pattern those of the maple tree and grow to a uniform height, making great leafy umbrellas in the woods. Their bright green leaves and white flowers—and shining red berries that appear later—enhance every spot in which they grow.

But beware! Every leaf rib is armed on the underneath side with sharp needle-like spines. And as if this were not enough, prickers also appear at random where there are no ribs. This spiking pattern is multiplied a hundredfold on the stems and stalks. The description *"horridus,"*

hairy

1 Queen's Cup
   Clintonia uniflora
2 Goatsbeard
   Aruncus dioicus

3 Bunchberry
   Cornus canadensis
4 Thimbleberry
   Rubus parviflorus

5 Red Columbine
   Aquilegia formosa
6 Foamflower
   Tiarella trifoliata

which translates as prickly porcupine, is not lightly used for this plant; it can be very painful if casually touched. The Indians used devil's club for many medicinal purposes, but they picked it only when the prickers were new and tender.

EXCHAMSIKS RIVER PROVINCIAL PARK
Yellowhead Highway

Exchamsiks River

Moving westward, the road begins to parallel the great Skeena River as it flows through its fjord. The river is mud brown from the turbulence of melting snows. Newly uprooted trees fill its rushing waters only to become stranded in its eddies and bars.

We drove until we reached Exchamsiks River Provincial Park. A cluster of old-growth spruce gives grandeur to this tiny park, but it is the Exchamsiks River, flowing on its three sides, that makes the park memorable. The combination of young green tree reflections and glacial-flowered water gives the river an incredible blue-green color. Along a nature trail near the river new flowers wait to be seen and painted. The delicate tall fringecup and slender Macoun's buttercup graced our park site. A few miles beyond the park the beautiful color of the Exchamsiks River vanishes upon joining the muddy waters of the Skeena.

As we continued to drive, the Skeena fjord grows ever more beautiful and interesting. The river widens and widens until it is almost a mile across. It is now salty on top and fresh underneath, responding to the tides that enter it. Salmon fishing is good here. Bald eagles appear. Gradually our road veers away from the river and we see it no more.

Skeena River in Spring - painting on pages 56–57

1 Yellow Monkey-flower
   Mimulus guttatus
2 Macoun's Buttercup
   Ranunculus macounii
3 Tall Fringecup, *Tellima grandiflora*
4 Wood Forget-me-not
   Myosotis sylvatica
5 Low Braya, *Braya humilis*

P.J. HAMMOND
Skeena River, B.C at peak

PRUDHOMME PROVINCIAL PARK
HAYS MOUNTAIN BOG
Prince Rupert

End of the Yellowhead Highway, British Columbia

We make Prudhomme Provincial Park our base for sightseeing in the area. It is a small, but exceptional park about fifteen miles east of Prince Rupert on the Yellowhead Highway. We prefer staying here and commuting into the city nearby. The first time we stopped at this park the flowers were all yellow. I painted them, but then sold my picture miles later when we met again an acquaintance from this park. This early sale left a hole in my flower portfolio that would take four years to fill. I was eagerly awaiting our arrival at Prudhomme on our second trip northward to Alaska. But alas, I was to find fewer yellow flowers this time: only yellow large-leaved geum and yellow hawkweed were blooming. Change, nature's gardener, had been at work. However, my discovery of the salal bush with its delightful small bells and evergreen foliage made up for this disappointment.

Our stay in the area included the gondola ride up Prince Rupert's Mt. Hays. We wanted to see the magnificent panoramic view of the area with mysterious Alaska lying in the distance and to walk the alpine bog at the top. Winding throughout the bog is a small boardwalk protecting the fragile ecology. The Jeffrey's shooting star, white mountain heather, bog blueberry, skunk cabbage, and white marsh marigold were exquisite in their spring newness. Cotton grass, seen in the bogs of Newfoundland and Maine, also flourished here.

We unexpectedly met some new friends from Prudhomme whose daughter is a marine biologist in the city. She was also a photographer of wildflowers. She introduced me to Lewis Clark's small field guide, *Wild Flowers of Marsh and Waterway in the Pacific Northwest*, which added greatly to my ability to recognize the names of the flowers in this region.

Time is needed to enjoy the smallness of alpine plants. The white broad-leafed marsh marigold and occasional butterwort were new to me. At this point in my flower education, I thought butterworts were early spring violets until I studied and painted their unusual leaves. Anyone, whether a plant lover or not, will find inspiration from the delightful bog on top of Mt. Hays. And the spectacular view from this spot offers a prelude of what lies ahead for travelers on the Inside Passage.

We always come into Prince Rupert's Park Avenue Campground only the night before we are to leave. Because of its proximity to the ferry

1 Large-leaved Avens
  Geum macrophyllum
2 Salmonberry, *Rubus spectabilis*
3 Bunchberry, *Cornus canadensis*

4 Hawkweed, *Hieracium Sp.*
5 Wild Lily-of-the-Valley
  Maianthemum canadense
6 Salal, *Gaultheria shallon*

Prince Rupert, B.C.
Ridley Island

63

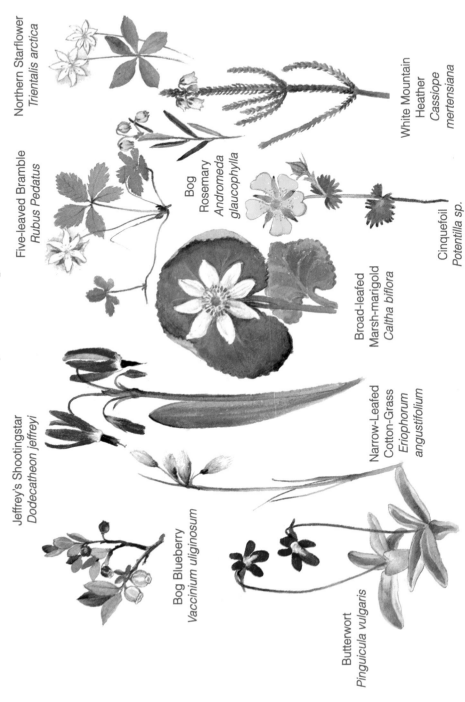

Mt. Hays, Prince Rupert

Northern Starflower
Trientalis arctica

White Mountain
Heather
*Cassiope
mertensiana*

Five-leaved Bramble
Rubus Pedatus

Bog
Rosemary
*Andromeda
glaucophylla*

Cinquefoil
Potentilla sp.

Broad-leafed
Marsh-marigold
Caltha biflora

Jeffrey's Shootingstar
Dodecatheon jeffreyi

Narrow-Leafed
Cotton-Grass
*Eriophorum
angustifolium*

Bog Blueberry
Vaccinium uliginosum

Butterwort
Pinguicula vulgaris

terminus, this park is a favorite with all boat travelers. Hardly an inch is vacant by early afternoon. It fills and empties with the rhythm of the ferry schedules.

Our Inside Passage ticket read Prince Rupert to Ketchikan, June 11, 9:00 A.M. The laundry was done; the motor home gas tank almost empty anticipating cheaper American prices; a great bald eagle watched from a nearby Sitka spruce. Waiting in line we moved onto the ferry. Our Alaskan adventure was about to begin!

The Observer

Ridley Island, Prince Rupert, B.C. - painting on pages 60–61

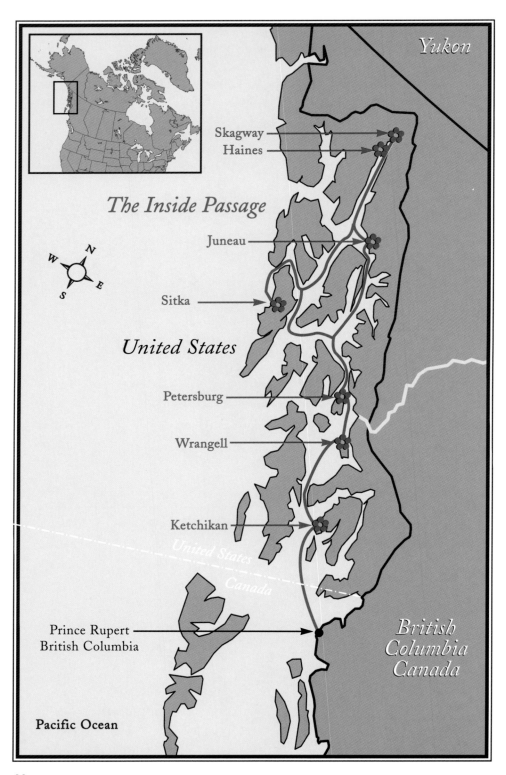

CHAPTER 4
INSIDE PASSAGE
Southeast Alaska

KETCHIKAN

WRANGELL

PETERSBURG

SITKA

JUNEAU

SKAGWAY

HAINES

Leaving Prince Rupert

Not long after leaving Prince Rupert, the Inside Passage spreads out like an inland sea. Despite its vastness and lack of habitation, there is a fleeting feeling of New England in the hue and timbered shapes of the distant shores. However, this impression quickly fades as one moves steadily northward. The hills grow into mountains, green gives way to white, and extraordinary islands burst out of the water in all shapes and sizes.

Suddenly after six hours of absolute wilderness, the bustle of Ketchikan appears. It lies like a colorful chain along the water's edge with mountains rising sharply behind it. Although Ketchikan is actually on an island, it gives every appearance of being part of the mainland. Its name comes from the Tlingit Indian word Kitschk-Hin, meaning the creek of the "thundering wings of an eagle." Over the loudspeaker of the ferry the words boom out, "You are approaching the sunshine capital of the world." Sunshine, indeed! The fact is that Ketchikan gets 162 inches of rain in an average year. Rainy Seattle's usual amount is 39 inches. We docked among fishing boats, giant blue and silver container boxes of incoming and outgoing products, and the general activity of a bustling community. Ketchikan is Alaska's fourth largest city, having about 8500 residents.

We stayed in two different parks: Signal Creek U.S. National Forest campground near town and Settlers Cove about twenty-five miles beyond it. Signal Creek is in the great rain forest of the Tongass National Forest, which covers over a million square miles along the region of the Inside Passage; sixty percent of the giant trees in this area are hemlock and thirty percent Sitka spruce. The park lies beside Ward Lake, which has an interesting nature trail around it and excellent biking on nearby dirt roads. Few flowers were blooming at the time of our visit.

It was a different scene at Settlers Cove, where we found many wildflowers and enjoyed a nature program presented by a Native American botanist. Under her guidance we discovered edible plants on the seashore: sea blite, chocolate lily, goose-tongue. (It was hard for me to believe that anyone could dig up the beautiful chocolate lily to eat its bulb!) Cow parsnip, salmonberry, buttercup, yellow money flower, shooting star, silverweed, and many other plants thronged the area.

At both ends of Ketchikan one finds totem parks. Here marvelous carved old Indian poles stand over seventy-five feet in the air. They recount, in painted red, black, and occasionally azure symbols, the history and legends of their people. The raven, the beaver, the salmon, and, yes, Abraham Lincoln and his Secretary of State, William Seward, appear on

1 Devil's Club
   Echinopanax horridum
2 Dwarf Fireweed
   Epilobium latifolium
3 Shooting Star
   Dodecatheon pulchellum
4 Chocolate Lily, Indian Rice
   Fritillaria camschatcensis
5 Silverweed, *Potentilla egedii*

these poles, sometimes favorably portrayed, sometimes not. Seward is upside down because he insulted the customs of hospitality by not bringing gifts to the Indians when he came to visit. Lincoln, deeply admired by the Indians, appears at the summit of some poles with his top hat on.

There was something in the spirit of Ketchikan that thrilled us on both our visits. It set the tone for our adventures on the waterway.

WRANGELL

In Wrangell we saw some of the largest and finest wildflowers of our whole trip. As we drove outside the city, glorious flowers nodded in colorful profusion on the shoulders of the roads. We had to stop to see them! Nearby was an easily accessible bog dotted with Labrador tea and sheep's laurel. Here I met deer cabbage for the first time.

Cruise ships do not come to Wrangell much. Perhaps this is because it has the smallest population of the major cities on the waterway. Without the coming and going of cruise-ship passengers, the city is much less frenzied almost like a city of an earlier period. We found old-fashioned bells for our bikes in Wrangell.

We biked and walked to the bridge leading to Chief Shakes Island, beautifully located amongst the fishing boats of the harbor. The Island's Indian community house, surrounded by unusual totems, reflects Wrangell's long Indian history.

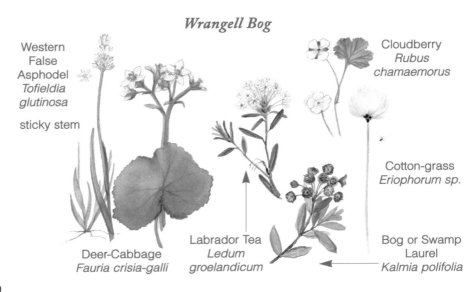

Wrangell Bog

Western False Asphodel
Tofieldia glutinosa

sticky stem

Cloudberry
Rubus chamaemorus

Cotton-grass
Eriophorum sp.

Deer-Cabbage
Fauria crisia-galli

Labrador Tea
Ledum groelandicum

Bog or Swamp Laurel
Kalmia polifolia

1 Dwarf Fireweed, *Epilobium latifolium*
2 Coneflower, *Centaurea cyanus*
3 Ox-eye Daisy
   Chrysanthemum leucanthemum

4 Western Columbine
   Aquilegia formosa
5 Yellow Hawkweed, *Hieracium triste*
6 White Clover, *Trifolium repens*

7 Orange Hawkweed
   Hieracium aurantiacum

PETERSBURG

The approach to Petersburg by ferry is through the Wrangell Narrows, a dredged area that shortens passage by one day. The captain on the bridge and a sailor on the bow watched carefully as we passed between the many channel markers. Because the buoy lights alternate red and green, the area is known as the Christmas-tree trail; and its appearance at night more than justifies this name. It is a delightful sight in the inky darkness of the Inside Passage's wilderness.

As we drew nearer to Petersburg in daylight on one of our trips, we passed through an area like no other on the Inside Passage. The channel was busy with small boats plying the waters. The shoreline was sprinkled with homesteads, cottages, and shacks. Two people from a tiny porch on the shore sent us semaphore signals with colorful sheets. A fisherman off our starboard held up a three-foot salmon for all to see. Everything was informal, festive, and relaxed.

Cruise ships do not berth in Petersburg. The residents voted against them some years ago. However, one sees here one of the most modern docking facilities in all of Alaska. The port is alive with the masts of salmon fishing boats—hundreds of them—and pleasure powerboats as well. I am sure there must have been pleasure boats in other port harbors, but this is the first time we noticed them.

Petersburg does not have the Native Indian population that other Alaskan cities have. It was started as a site for a cannery and sawmill, around 1900, by a Norwegian, Peter Buschmann. He invited his fellow Norwegians to join him and they became the city's population base.

Rainwear is a daily necessity in rain forests of the Inside Passage. Our experience has been of a constant light dew rather than heavy rain. It falls so gently on our vehicle's roof that I call it cat's paws. Clouds usually cover all but the lower parts of the mountains.

On our first trip those ever-present clouds lifted one afternoon and the sun came out. There beyond the boats' masts across the bay was another unimaginable view of snow and glaciers and peaks, all glowing in the lambent afternoon sunlight. However, I had only enough time to sketch the sky and mountains, but not the water, because we were due at the ferry in the next few minutes. On our return trip four years later, I added the water and harbor foreground to the picture. But the weather never allowed us see that magnificent view of the mountains again.

Unfortunately, we could not control our time in Petersburg on any of our visits, the ferry did. We never seemed to have enough time to explore for flowers; those we did see were like the ones I had already recorded. By making reservations early one can plan the time desired in each port, but somehow our program for Petersburg was always sacrificed to the ferry planners. My hope is to return again to gracious Petersburg and see that mountain view once more, perhaps in afternoon sunlight.

Petersburg

SITKA

Sitka, situated on Baranof Island, is fourteen hours by ferry from either Petersburg or Juneau. Located on the Pacific Ocean, it is a site rich in history. Originally inhabited by Tlingit Indians, Sitka became the capital of Russian Alaska in 1808. It was here in 1867 that the United States took possession of Alaska.

As we left the ferry, we turned north away from the city towards the U.S. Forest Service's Starrigavan campground. From this base, we would commute daily into Sitka. The park is in an old-growth forest with a second section across the road, on the water. It offers hiking, clamming, a fish watch, and excellent biking on an old mining road between the mountains.

The flowers I have selected come from various parts of the island. The American brooklime is from our own campsite; the Alaska paintbrush and wintercress grace the sides of the road that goes to the airport on Japonski Island; the pink and white Siberian spring beauties, whose leaves were often eaten, raw or cooked, by the natives, can be seen in the Sitka National Historical Park.

This lovely, quiet park commemorates the defeat of the Tlingit Indians at the hands of the Russians. It has an interpretive center where information about this event is presented. There is also a walk lined with many superb old and new totem poles that reveal the great individuality of the carvers. The forest is alive with ravens yodeling back and forth high in the great Sitka spruce trees. I have noted that wherever you have a strong Indian presence in Alaska, you have an abundance of ravens. This is not surprising when one realizes that the Indians revered this bird above all other birds and animals. In their rich culture the raven was the creative force. We had not noticed any ravens in Petersburg. Could this be because there appears to be no Indian tradition behind that area?

Nearby is the Sheldon Jackson Museum, said to have the finest collection of native arts and crafts in Alaska. Browsing through the many drawers of artifacts, one gains a much deeper appreciation of the culture and achievements of native peoples.

Although Sitka seems like the last possible place you would expect to find a superb international group of chamber musicians, it has one in summer. To slip in for a free rehearsal after a busy day of sightseeing or to attend one of their evening concerts is like putting a crown on a visit to this small historical city.

1 American Brooklime
  Veronica americana
2 Alaska Paintbrush
  Castilleja unalaschensis

3 Rockcress, *Arabis sp*
4 Wintercress, *Barbarea orthoceras*
5 Siberian Spring Beauty
  Claytonia Sibirica

Looking out on beautiful Crescent Bay with its marvelous volcanic island, cruise ships, and mysterious cloud-shrouded mountains, one finds it easy to imagine what this sheltered harbor must have looked like years ago when Russian ships and native canoes dotted the waters.

JUNEAU

There are only two ways to reach the capital of Alaska—by boat or plane. Until one actually approaches Juneau, this fact is hard to grasp. As the city comes into view from the water, one sees two great snow-capped mountains with a colossal sea of ice between them. This frozen mass is the Mendenhall Glacier. It dwarfs everything around it. Truly, it is an awesome sight!

The ferry docks thirteen miles north of Juneau. We hurried to the U.S. Forest Service campground on Mendenhall Lake because it is almost always full. Its location across from the face of the glacier makes it a most popular camping site. Wooded and secluded, with a small bog, the park has a great diversity of wildflowers. The bog candles or tall white bog orchids were outstanding on one visit. I saw step moss, red stemmed feather moss, and three hands, *Peltigera aphthosa,* for the first time here. Pink pyrolas grew by the campsite. At the lake's edge another whole group of flowers blossomed.

To the tourist Juneau means the Mendenhall Glacier. Over 120,000 visitors come each year to see it. When it was first discovered by John Muir over one hundred years ago, it was a tidal glacier. Today the face of the glacier has retreated fifteen miles from the ocean.

One of the things that I love most about this glacier is that it provides such a laboratory for learning how nature re-establishes itself after the ice withdraws. First, there is only the fine sand and silt of the terminal moraine. As the glacier continues to retreat slowly, mosses and sedges start to grow on the silt and sand, building up the soil. With more time, and with increased distance from the ice face, horsetails, swale grass, and alders appear, along with a few flowers such as fireweed and yarrow. Still further back from the glacier, seedling spruce and dogwood shrubs grab hold. It is hard to realize that where the Visitors' Center is today, there was once only a sea of ice, so natural is the vegetation surrounding it.

1 Beach Pea, *Lathyrus maritimus*
2 Red Twig Dogwood
  Cornus stolonifera
3 Common Sedge, *Carex aquatatis.*
4 Tall Willowherb, *Epilobium sp.*
5 Haircap Moss
  Plagiomnium drummondii

6 Brome Grass, *Bromus sp.*
7 Three Hands, *Peltigera aphthosa*
8 Nagoonberry, *Rubus arcticus*
9 *Cladonia cariosa*
10 *Pleurozium schreberi*
11 *Sphagnum moss sp.*
12 *Hylocomium splendens*

We spent a day driving north of Juneau on the Glacier Highway; we stopped at Eagle Beach en route. The view of the Chilkat mountain range across the Favorite Channel is the type only Alaska can provide. Cow parsnips were huge along this road and at the beach edge. In the tangle of plants along the shore, chocolate lily and beach pea grew.

Cruise ships dock in old Juneau, as many as three at a time. Another might be out in the bay with four or more seaplanes drawn up to it. Passengers throng this section of the city. The Red Dog Saloon is always full! Juneau was founded on gold. In 1880 two prospectors, Joe Juneau and Dick Harris, detected the metal in a small stream which ran through the center of present-day Juneau. This event was to lead to the discovery of one of the largest lodes of gold quartz in the world.

We spent a day in Juneau on our first visit, four days on our second. I am never satisfied with our time in Juneau. There is just so much to see.

SKAGWAY

We have been to Skagway twice, once by water taxi from Haines and once by way of the Alaskan Highway at Jake's Corner through Carcross and the White Pass. It is hard to imagine, as one drives so easily through the pass today, what a horrible obstacle this steep pass was in 1897 for the thousands headed for the Klondike gold fields.

The first boatload of gold prospectors or stampeders, as they were called, arrived in July of 1897. Some went on the Chilkoot trail out of nearby Dyea, others chose the White Pass out of Skagway. Their goal was to reach Lake Bennett, where they built boats to float on the Yukon River to Dawson City and the gold fields beyond; 30,000 came, 5000 in February of 1898 alone. In May of that year the building of the White Pass Railroad started and was quickly finished. By 1899 the gold rush was over.

Skagway has reinvented itself. It is again a place of great activity —this time tourist activity. On a clear day the roar of helicopters coming and going continues as long as there is light. The proximity of glaciers, mountains, and Glacier Bay National Park lures many sightseers skyward. The blasts of steam whistles echo through the small valley, announcing tourist excursions on the still active White Pass and Yukon Railroad to the top of the pass to see the reminders of the old gold rush days.

Skagway

1 Prickly Rose, *Rosa acicularis*
2 Common Harebell
Campanula rotundifolia
3 Western Columbine
Aquilegia formosa.

4 Pink Pyrolla, *Pyrola asarifolia*
5 Coastal Paintbrush
Castilleja unalaschensis
6 Beach Pea, *Lathyrus maritimus*
7 Satin Flower, *Godetia sp.*

Skagway

The town is a regular port-of-call for cruise ships. It is not unusual to see two or three tied up at once. Often a freighter lies waiting for the great ore trucks with their loads of zinc. These come through the pass from the Yukon. The Inside Passage Ferry docks almost every day and sometimes twice a day in summer. The tide of people swells and ebbs in Skagway with the movement of the ships.

In many ways Skagway still maintains its old ambiance—wooden boardwalks, the Red Onion Saloon, museums, and small shops selling excellent native products. On the outskirts of town there is an old cemetery where graves of the early pioneers may be seen, including those of the villainous Soapy Smith and Frank Reed who shot him. Skagway gives wonderful insights into a brief moment of history that was both colorful and wild.

Some of my flowers were gathered from the old road to Dyea. This tent city of thousands lost its prestige to nearby Skagway when the railroad was built and the boats became too large for its tidal basin. Today

White Pass (Skagway)

there is only a sign to commemorate the past town site. However, its disappearance has been a boon for wildflowers. The pyrola and columbine I depict come from the woods beside the road; the others, from the shore area. I learned later that the satin flower was a garden escapee.

Haines was our last stop on the Inside Passage and seems to be the sunniest of all the ports we have visited in the rain forest. Its setting, with glorious mountains almost encircling it, their nunataks* and white glaciers, great cragged peaks leaping into the trumpeting blue sky, puts this area into a category of beauty all by itself. Nearby is the Chilkat River where, from October to January, one can see the largest concentration of bald eagles in the world. More than 3000 migrate to this spot for the late chum salmon run. We lingered in Haines.

We met "Knute" Knutson in his woodworking shop; we ate salmon at the salmon bake; we did our laundry. We bought our fishing license in Haines. We fished, watched eagles fish, biked, hiked, bought Dungeness crab.

There are two state parks in this area—Chilkoot and Chilkat. Chilkat satisfies my desire to camp in a setting of beauty. On each visit we have been fortunate to be among the great trees beside the blue-green Chilkat Lake; there are only a few campsites next to the water. I love to paint here. We also spent time at the less frequented Chilkoot Park about fifteen miles away.

In this park we hiked a wooded trail to see a great field of wild-flowers dancing in the wind near the ocean. The woods were dotted with the charming single delight, a plant about three or four inches high with a solitary bloom. I was surprised to see them. I did not think anything could bloom in so dark a forest. When we left the woods for sunlight, we found ourselves in a field bursting with glorious wildflowers up to the waist and higher. Wild geranium, columbine, iris, cow parsnip, and many others vied for our attention. We hiked out to the water's edge to enjoy the hanging glacier on the opposite shore of the inlet. We noted that the the snow in the mountains was much less than on our trips in 1988 and 1992, the glacier much retreated. Perhaps we were seeing the effects of global warming; perhaps it was only the normal variation of the seasons.

It is always with much regret that we say goodbye to Haines and the Inside Passage, but then so much still lay before us.

---

* Nunataks is an Eskimo word for the bare rock peaks which appear above the high mountain ice and snow.

Hanging Glacier, Chilcoot Bay

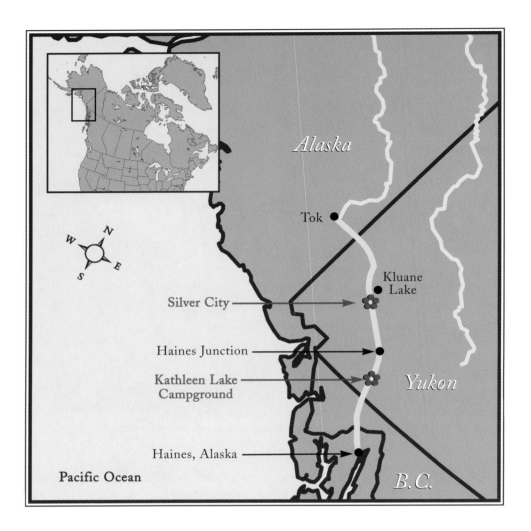

CHAPTER 5
YUKON CONNECTION
Yukon, Canada

Kluane National Park Reserve

KATHLEEN LAKE CAMPGROUND
Haines Highway
Yukon Highway 3

SILVER CITY
Milepost 1023
Alaska Highway 1

The Vastness of the Yukon

KATHLEEN LAKE CAMPGROUND
Kluane National Park Reserve
Haines Highway
Yukon Highway 3

The Haines Highway is the general name for the road that connects Haines, the terminus of the Inside Passage ferry, with Haines Junction on the Alaska Highway. It starts in south Alaska, quickly enters British Columbia, then passes into the Yukon. The highway covers 151 miles of absolutely awesome country. Canada's highest mountain range, the St. Elias with its many peaks over 17,000 feet, parallels the road on the left as you drive northward. The extraordinary configurations of snow and rock suggest great flowing figures dancing up and down the ridges. Glacial flats, where rivers braid and unbraid like ribbons, join the road.

The vastness of the Yukon spreads out before us. We have entered "the land of little sticks," an appellation that comes from translation of the Russian word "taiga," and a phenomenon of northern regions around the globe—Scandinavia, Russia, Siberia, Alaska, Canada. According to the botanists, spruce and fir trees, which may be decades old, are stunted because of the muskeg or permafrost on which they grow. I prefer to think the trees grow this way so that we can have an unobstructed view of the grandeur, order, and beauty of a great creator. Thousands of dwarf trees, worthless to the logger, fill the valley with endless rhythms and designs, patterns of beauty delighting the eye.

Kathleen Lake is one of three or four campgrounds in this wilderness region and the only designated one within the vast Kluane National Park Reserve. Its campsites are relatively high and dry, with wildflowers totally different from those of its lake basin. Around the campsites one sees bedstraw, arnica, and the many flowers that flourish in drier soil and sunlight. This contrasts with the flora in the boggy woods down by the lake. There crowberry and kinnikinnick mat earth's floor, and four-parted gentian find such suitable moisture that they achieve a fullness of flowering I have not seen before. The park is unforgettable in its explosion of plant varieties.

Kathleen Lake, from which the park gets its name, is glacial-fed and a stunning turquoise. By taking a beach trail around the small peninsula, one gains a good view of the lake's size and extraordinary color. There is only one spot on the road, from the northern approach, where this colorful lake can be seen. Good hiking trails, some on boardwalks, make the viewing of flowers most pleasant, but beware of mosquitoes!

1 Hairy Arnica, *Arnica alpina*
2 Single Delight, *Moneses uniflora*
3 Four-parted Gentian
  Gentiana propinqua
4 Siberian Aster, *Aster sibiricus*

5 Kinnikinnick, *Arctostaphylos uva-ursi*
6 Northern Bedstraw
  Galium boreale
7 Cinquefoil, *Potentilla sp.*
8 Crowberry, *Empetrum nigrum*

We found almost no visitors in the parks of this area on any of our trips. The highway is excellent! It is surprising that more people have not discovered the specialness of this region.

Colors of the Yukon

SILVER CITY
Kluane National Park Reserve
Milepost 1023
Alaska Highway 1

The turnoff for Silver City is immediately after one's first glimpse of Kluane Lake, (pronounced kloo-WA-nee), the Yukon's largest lake. Today the "city" is a small cluster of decaying log buildings, trees growing up in them, ground squirrels inhabiting them. However, every tour bus makes a stop at this historic site. In the early 1900s miners traded here on their way to the Kluane Lake placer-gold fields, and Canadian mounted police were posted here to maintain law and order. By 1925 only one person still lived at this site. The area saw a temporary revival of activity in 1943 as log barracks were added to house the men working on the Fairbanks/Haines pipeline and a new road. The building of the Alaska Highway or Alcan, as it is commonly called, had become a national war priority; the Japanese were landing on the Aleutian Islands.

As neglected as this site is by humans, wildflowers abound. In 1992 we saw pea flowers and oxytropes lining the three-mile gravel approach road. There have been so many special flowers in this spot that we try to stop every time we pass. Jacob's ladder, Sudan's lousewort, cut-leaf anemone, and mountain bluebell are some of the flowers seen here. For best viewing of wildflowers at this milepost, one should be here by late June, and if the sun is shining, there is a superb view of the famous green-blue of Kluane Lake from beyond the shacks. The glorious color of so many of the glacier-fed lakes and rivers of this region comes from the presence of glacial flour in their waters. Particles from the melting of glaciers become suspended in the waters and reflect the blue light rays of the sunlight. The colors resulting from this phenomenon always fill me with wonder.

Kluane National Park Reserve is very special. This was universally recognized when, in 1980, it became a joint UNESCO World Heritage Site, along with the Wrangell-St. Elias National Park in Alaska.

hairy

1 Heartleaf Arnica
  Arnica cordifolia
2 Cut-leaf Anemone
  Anemone multifida
3 Death Camas
  Zygadnus elegans

4 Sudan's Lousewort
  Pedicularis sudetica
5 Tall Lungwort
  Mertensia paniculata
6 Jacob's Ladder
  Polemonium pulcherrimum

1 Siberian Aster
  Aster sibiricus
2 Mountain Goldenrod
  Solidago multiradiata
3 Arctic Lupine
  Lupinus arcticus

4 Pink Pyrola
  Pyrola asarifolia
5 Pink Common Yarrow
  Achillea millefolium
6 Nagoonberry
  Rubus arcticus

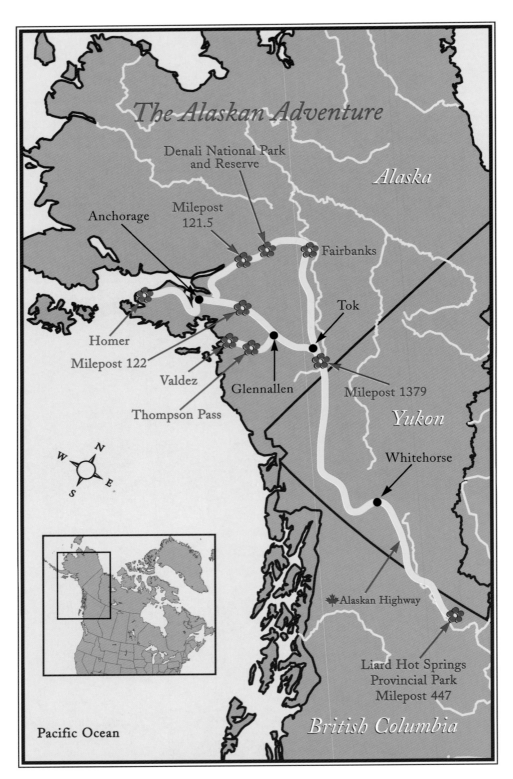

The Alaskan Adventure

Denali National Park and Reserve

Alaska

Milepost 121.5

Anchorage

Fairbanks

Tok

Homer

Milepost 122

Valdez

Glennallen

Thompson Pass

Milepost 1379

Yukon

Whitehorse

N
W   E
S

Alaskan Highway

Liard Hot Springs
Provincial Park
Milepost 447

British Columbia

Pacific Ocean

CHAPTER 6
THE ALASKAN ADVENTURE

Central Alaska

THOMPSON PASS
Richardson Highway

MINERAL CREEK ROAD
Valdez, end of Richardson Highway

MILEPOST 122
Glenn Highway

THE ROAD TO HOMER
Sterling Highway

MILEPOST 121.5
George Parks Highway

DENALI NATIONAL PARK AND RESERVE
George Parks Highway

Going Out—Leaving Alaska
FAIRBANKS
Milepost 1523
End of the Alaska Highway

MILEPOST 1379
Alaska Highway 2

LIARD HOT SPRINGS PROVINCIAL PARK
Milepost 447
Highway 97
British Columbia, Canada

Farewell to the Yukon - painting on pages 90-91

THOMPSON PASS

16 miles east of Valdez, Richardson Highway

Thompson Pass is not the highest pass in Alaska; it ranks only ninth, but it holds all records for snowfall south of the Arctic Circle— 974 inches for a season, 62 inches in a 24-hour period. In June the pass is a wildflower paradise. The Alpine plants grow in such variety and exquisiteness that it is almost unbelievable.

Each time we reached the summit as we traveled towards Valdez, we absolutely had to pull into the first available turnout in order to absorb the wonder of the Chugach Mountains, flowing range after range before us with their endless nunataks jutting above the snow and glaciers. When we had our fill of this extraordinary sight, we drove a few hundred yards to the next drive-out for more. Here we discovered a path leading out to a nearby ridge from which one can view still another panoramic scene, this time of the valley leading down towards Valdez. On this path one can also safely view the flowers without disturbing the tundra.

As we hiked out, the earth was still wet and brown in places where the snow had just melted, but flowers were already bursting into bloom. There were colonies of mountain heather, bearberry, anemone, plants less than an inch high, many only six inches. I hardly recognized a plant. Everything was in miniature. I simply sat down and started to paint what I saw. Names could come later. I felt as though I could have stayed here forever, but alas, I have a partner whose middle name is "move on."

Our first trip to Valdez through the pass was in complete fog. We had no idea we had missed anything. All we could see were the tall snow poles, which looked ridiculously high to two Vermonters. It was not until we were leaving Valdez a few days later that we glimpsed what the fog had enshrouded.

We had decided to spend our last night in the area at Blueberry State Park just below the top of the pass. It was about 9:30 in the evening when we finally left the city. Suddenly we caught a glimpse of the Chugach Mountains above us. The slanting rays of the sun bathed them in purest light. We stopped as often as we dared, along the road, taking photographs of that endless white range. Then we hurried on to the park.

We had learned about Blueberry Park from The Milepost, the Alaskan travelers' bible. It has been described as Alaska's most beautiful park, the Switzerland of Alaska! There are no signs marking its presence, perhaps because it is so small. I sensed if we could reach it before the fog, which was now rolling in like a locomotive, we would see something

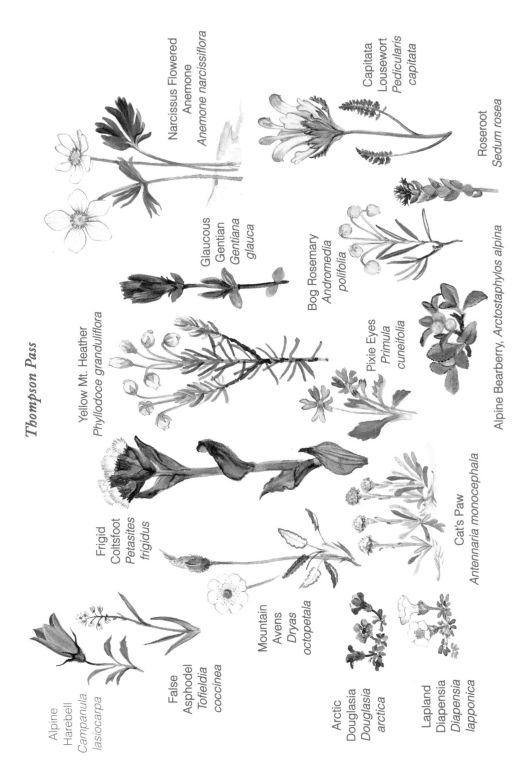

Thompson Pass

Alpine Harebell
Campanula lasiocarpa

False Asphodel
Tofieldia coccinea

Arctic Douglasia
Douglasia arctica

Lapland Diapensia
Diapensia lapponica

Mountain Avens
Dryas octopetala

Frigid Coltsfoot
Petasites frigidus

Yellow Mt. Heather
Phyllodoce granduliflora

Cat's Paw
Antennaria monocephala

Pixie Eyes
Primula cuneifolia

Glaucous Gentian
Gentiana glauca

Bog Rosemary
Andromedia polifolia

Narcissus Flowered Anemone
Anemone narcissiflora

Capitata Lousewort
Pedicularis capitata

Roseroot
Sedum rosea

Alpine Bearberry, *Arctostaphylos alpina*

wonderful. However, there was to be only the briefest glimpse of the sunlit mountains from the park before they were lost in the swirling clouds. In the morning the wildflowers outside our door were a complement to our experience higher up in the pass. I have since learned that here we were surrounded by Capitata lousewort, Lapland diapensia, frigid coltsfoot, glaucous gentian. Before we had to leave this exquisite park, the clouds swirled away and we were permitted to see its mountain views. Unforgettable!

So much of the pleasure in our lives seems to come from special moments when weather, light, location, nature, and our receptiveness join hands in perfect harmony. I have certainly had my share of these moments in Thompson Pass!

MINERAL CREEK ROAD
Valdez

The scenic Mineral Creek Road is perhaps not what most people come to Valdez to see. A boat trip to the Columbia Glacier, a tour of the Alyeska Pipeline Marine Terminus, fishing for salmon on Winnebago Point are generally far more popular. Certainly the boat trip to see marine life and the Columbia glacier in Prince William Sound has to be the high point of any visit to Valdez. This tidewater glacier with its icebergs is spectacular, but if one has time, investigating the scenic Mineral Creek Road can be an enriching experience as well. It is a microcosm of many of the facets that one associates with the Alaskan adventure.

The approach to this road is by an old bridge. Since our first trip to this spot was in a small motor home, we had no trouble driving across on the old plank bridge. However, on later trips with a larger vehicle, it seemed wiser to park on the near side of it and to bike and hike in. There are great thundering falls to be seen, a wonderful hanging glacier, a mining dredge working the stream bed. I joined a couple from Missouri panning for gold in a quiet eddy of the boisterous river that flows through the valley and had my first lesson in this art! I discovered that there are easier ways of making money than washing gold specks out of sand.

Wildflowers abound here, encouraged by the rain forest climate. My first discovery of Sitka valerian was on this road. It resembles New England heliotrope and grows high over one's head. Wild geraniums flowered in tangles with roses, cow parsnips, and oxytropses. The small northern goldenrod grew on the edge of the road. We have been to Valdez three times, and each time have been drawn to explore the out of the way Mineral Creek Road.

hairy

1 Wild Geranium, *Geranium erianthum*
2 Sitka Valerien, *Valerian sitchensis*
3 Northern Goldenrod, *Solidago multiradiata*

4 Prickly Rose, *Rosa acicularis*
5 Northern Oxytrope
  Oxytropis campestris

One of the wonderful provisions for highway travel in Alaska are the large paved and double-ended turnouts on the roads. They give an opportunity to travelers, particularly those in trailers and motor homes, to rest and a place to stay overnight when no towns or facilities are near-by. Usually a motor home draws in for the evening about 5:00; by 8:00 there may be three or four more drawn up for the night. The cluster of vehicles provides a sense of safety to all, as well as opportunities to exchange news and information. British Columbia has outlawed this type of parking; the Yukon frowns upon it strongly; Alaska alone still permits it.

Milepost 122 is just such a stopping spot with an excellent view of Gunsight Mountain to the west. Below the road the land falls away into a series of small connecting lakes, giving this area great enchantment. The site was very special to me because of the flowers I had painted there on an earlier trip. I was eagerly looking forward to rechecking them. But alas, in 1995 all had vanished. The road was torn up, being changed into a thruway, and for miles on either side everything was ripped apart.

Unfortunately the road builders in Alaska are not content to do a small section and finish it. They have to tear up twenty or thirty miles and never finish anything. This year we saw so many motor homes with Alaskan license plates that we thought, naively as it turned out, that at last the people of this great state were really enjoying it. On the contrary, the motor homes were rented by "outsiders" who had learned about the road conditions and left their own vehicles at home. Not one highway escaped the road-building fever in Alaska. It seemed that every major road was in a state of partial upheaval. I think what disturbed visitors the most about the roads was the feeling that adequate roads were being changed on such a scale. Every grade was being modified, every curve straightened, the shoulders of the road broadened beyond reason. And for what? By standards in the lower forty-eight states, for a piddling bit of traffic!

Perhaps Milepost 122 will be restored. However, the lovely flea-bane daisy, tall Jacob's ladder, and *Capitate valerian*, which also contribut-ed to making this spot special, are probably gone from here forever. The reconstruction of the road shoulders is seldom done with indigenous seed.

hairy

1 Iceland Poppy, *Papaver nudicaule*
2 Capitate Valerian, *Valeriana capitata*
3 Tall Jacob's Ladder
   Polemonium acutiflorum

4 Bitter Fleabane, *Erigeron acris*
5 Black-tipped Groundsel
   Senecio lugens
6 *Papaver sp.*

THE ROAD TO HOMER
Sterling Highway

As far as I am concerned, the road to Homer begins when the Sterling Highway first starts to parallel the great Cook Inlet. Actually one makes the decision to go to Homer eighty-nine miles earlier, at exquisite Tern Lake, where the choice is made between going to Seward or Homer.

Before reaching Clam Gulch and the first view of the inlet, with the Aleutian chain of mountains running the length of it, one drives through Soldotna. This city, with the oil refineries to the north and the great salmon river, the Kenai, on its doorstep, is a frenetic area. It is a good place to grocery-shop and put in provisions because large supermarkets do not exist below this point. It is also about here that one should give careful consideration to the weather, which plays such an important part in one's enjoyment of the drive down the coast. On a clear day, after passing Clam Gulch, one can see the Aleutians fifty miles across the bright blue Inlet—sometimes erupting, sometimes smoking, but always glimmering white with pale blue shadows. The view is made even more unforgettable by the presence of spectacular Redoubt and Iliamna, two volcanic mountains of magnificent size in the mountain chain.

Sadly, one of the delights of driving to Homer is fast disappearing —camping anywhere one wishes along the precipitous cliff that plunges hundreds of feet straight down to the water's edge. It seems that the crowds coming to Alaska in the summer are necessitating more regulations as to where it is lawful to stop.

We made a small detour to see Ninilchik's native village and the old Russian Orthodox church that sits on a hill overlooking the great inlet. In some ways this area seems untouched by time. However, nearby Ninilchik River is becoming more and more popular as a fishing area and the old-fashioned look may change. A walking tour brochure helps visitors to better understand the community. This side trip was especially rewarding to me because here I saw large clumps of red Sitka burnets. I had seen the green variety throughout Alaska, but never the red species. Also, I recognized the Nootka lupine here.

One question asked of most visitors to this state is, "Did you go to Homer?" The first insight as to why this is asked can be gained just before the road plunges down into Homer. At this spot on the right is one of the most beautiful wide-angle views in all of Alaska. The lupines and giant white cow parsnips in the foreground, the pale yellow of the Homer spit slicing into the blue of the ocean, the snow-white Kenai

1 Dwarf Fireweed, *Epilobium latifolium*
2 Cotton-Grass, *Eriophorum sp.*
3 Sitka Burnet, *Sanguisorba officianalis*
4 Nootka Lupine, *Lupinus nootkatensis*
5 Wild Geranium, *Geranium erianthum*

Mountains beyond—all conspire to make this view unforgettable. The second reason is what the spit offers: delightful small shops, delicious seafood, great fishing (especially for halibut), and marvelous space for camping and parking—some of it free! And finally there is Homer itself. The Pratt Museum is a gem; it includes a most remarkable Alaskan wildflower garden with the plants all carefully labeled. The art galleries are admirable, filled with superb native work. And then there is the Skyline Drive which spoils you with another magnificent view, this time of Kachemak Bay with glaciers and mountains beyond. You will surely want to be able to say, "Yes, I have been to Homer!"

MILEPOST 121.5
George Parks Highway

We always look forward to stopping at this large double-ended rest area, which greets the visitor for miles in advance with large drifts of fireweed on either side of the road. This oasis has a small trail that offers a glimpse of the great Chulitna river as it braids across the valley. We always enjoy stopping here to stretch our legs and see what changes nature has brought.

The undergrowth is so lush that it reminds us of the rain forests of the Inside Passage. Spiny devil's club competes with cow parsnips eight feet tall; fireweed spires tower over my head. I never cease to marvel at how the gentle, but deadly monkshood can thread its way up to the sunlight amongst such aggressive neighbors. I am amazed that twisted stalk and roses thrive along the overgrown path.

A few miles beyond this spot one climbs the last rise, which gives the first grand view of the Alaska Range with its crown jewel, Denali Mountain. In the near distance the Ruth glacier reveals its face as it continues to retreat back up its fjord. On a clear day this sight is unforgettable. We have seen it only once and then very briefly. Weather is such a factor in the Alaskan canvas.

1 Twisted Stalk
  Streptopus amplexifolius
2 Monkshood
  Aconitum delphinifolium
3 Cow Parsnip, *Heracleum lanatum*

4 Twin Flower, *Linnaea borealis*
5 Cow Vetch, *Vicia cracca*
6 Devil's Club, *Echinopanax horridum*
7 Common Dandelion
  Taraxacum officinale

DENALI NATIONAL PARK & RESERVE
George Parks Highway

Denali National Park means different things to different people. For the majority it is wildlife; for some it is wilderness hiking; for an elite few it is the challenge of climbing Denali mountain; for me it is wildflowers, and then there's the moment when the afternoon sun dazzles the mountains in unimaginable colors!

Everyone enters the park with hopes of glimpsing the "high one," the meaning of the Tanana Indian word *Denali*. Unfortunately only about twenty percent of the thousands of yearly visitors see the peak. It is so high—20,320 feet—that it makes its own weather.

I first glimpsed the mountain hanging like a great white dome above the road as we traveled from Anchorage. From then on I would see it only shrouded in heavy clouds. On our second visit in 1992, we had fog down to the ground! I was unprepared, however, for the effect it would have on me when I finally did see it. It was in 1995, the last day of our third visit to the park, and there it was in all its magnificence. I could not believe my eyes. I could not believe any mountain could so dwarf its surroundings. I was overwhelmed by the tremendous size of its base—its complexity, ramparts, ravines, glaciers, glistening whites and pearlized blue shadows, the way it grew out of the earth. As I sat gazing, caribou grazed a few feet away, people mingled quietly, cameras clicked. Buses came and went.

The park is so vast that only a small fraction of its six million acres can be experienced by the visitor. I had just returned from a vigorous ranger-led hike and was strolling the road waiting for a bus to pick me up. The wildflowers were abundant and growing in such profusion that I kept going from one side of the road to the other so as not to miss any. Suddenly I saw a small white gentian. It was so fresh and unusual that I immediately sat down on the tundra to sketch it. As I worked, I began to understand more fully the purpose of this great park: it was to share itself, to enrich its guests with all the wonder of the qualities it so uniquely expressed. It did not matter where you came from, what your status in life might be, or where you were going—all would leave Denali the richer for their visit.

View from Eielson Visitors' Center

Denali
Visitors' Center and Savage River

1 Siberian Aster, *Aster sibiricus*
2 Pink Corydalis
   Corydalis sempervirens
3 Pink Plumes, *Polygonia bistorta*
4 Grass of Parnassus
   Parnassia palustris

5 Whirled Lousewort
   Pedicularis verticillata
6 Net-leaf Willow
   Salix reticulata
7 Red Bearberry
   Arctostaphylos rubra

Denali
Polychrome area

1 Frigid Arnica, *Arnica frigida*
2 Larkspur, *Delphinium glacum*
3 Moss Gentian, *Gentiana prostrata*
4 Arctic Sandwort
   Minartia macrocarpa

5 Death Camos
   Zygadenus elegans
6 Whitish Gentian, *Gentiana algida*
7 Fireweed
   Epilobium angustifolium

Going Out

FAIRBANKS
Milepost 1523
End of the Alaska Highway 1

For us one of the most noticeable attributes of Fairbanks is its clement weather. Each time we arrive in the city, we feel a softness to the air reminiscent of our own northern New England climate. We always remove our sweaters in Fairbanks. However, we were informed that our weather observation was not based on fact. We were told that the city actually has very hot summers with long hours of daylight and extremely harsh cold winters. The long warm growing season undoubtedly helps explain the presence in this location of the Agricultural and Forestry Experiment Station and the Georgeson Botanical Gardens.

The riotous colors of these gardens can be easily seen from the road. The gardens have many experimental plots of flowers and vegetables, all carefully labeled as to species and genus with the thought of finding what grows best in Alaska. Many volunteers maintain the gardens in beautiful order throughout the summer. By the first of August we can see some corn already in tassel, cabbages over a foot wide and growing, and raspberries, luscious and ripe. There is a large section of tall hybrid lilies in the most subtle and unusual shades, certainly the envy of any gardener. I must confess as might be expected that it is the four small plots of wildflowers that charm me the most.

We were on Sheep Creek Road on our last visit when a 95-car freight train, passing on its way to Anchorage, reminded me that a botanist friend once told me that railroad beds were excellent places to discover wildflowers, especially non-native ones. We found cow vetch, yellow sweet clover, and bur marigold, all importations, near the tracks. Across the road and up the bank, where the vegetation had not been disturbed, were hosts of bog flowers. Glorious examples of the tall yellow and plummy marsh fleabane thrive in the road ditches of this area.

Alaskan wildflower lovers are especially sensitive to the influx of non-native plants because they often overwhelm indigenous varieties. The U.S. Government's policy of subsidizing the planting of wildflowers along the highways in Alaska has been a mixed blessing. Because this state does not have sufficient quantity of native seed, the re-vegetation of roadsides has been carried on with whatever seed is available from the lower forty-eight states, often to the detriment of native flower populations. Steps are now being taken to correct this, but because Alaska is a

1 Marsh Fleabane
  Senecio congestus
2 Common Sow Thistle
  Sonchus oleraceus
3 Bunchberry
  Cornus canadensis

4 Hooded Ladies Tresses
  Spiranthes romanzoffiana
5 Bur Marigola, *Bidens laevis*
6 Lowbush Cranberry
  Vaccinium vitis-idaea
7 Labrador Tea, *Ledum palustris*

state whose plant population is predominantly perennial in nature, it may be years before a sufficient quantity of indigenous seed is available.

Later that day we drove out to Coombs Farm. This dairy of earlier years is now a wildlife sanctuary where, among other things, one can watch the banding of birds. The farmhouse with its museum gives a good insight into the early farming efforts of this region.

There are many things for the tourist to do and discover in Fairbanks. We panned for gold, enjoyed a river boat on the Chena and Tanana Rivers, dined at the Alaska Salmon Bake, enjoyed Alaskaland (designed to introduce guests to the history of interior Alaska), and visited the remarkable museum of the University of Alaska. We think all these activities are "musts," but each person finds his own experience in the city of Fairbanks.

MILEPOST 1379
Alaska Highway 1

We are now 141 miles from Fairbanks with views of the Mentasta mountains before and after this milepost. It is of no matter that we have never seen these grand mountains on a clear day. The changing clouds and endless mysterious shades of blue are always satisfying. They make me think of Japanese prints where mountains grade with lessening degrees of intensity as they fade into the distance.

This milepost with its very large turnout is unique for its wild-flowers, or at least it was until our most recent visit. A road crew has transformed the lower section into a gravel pit. And yet even in that inhospitable area we found masses of yellow dryas seeding the surroundings into a better soil condition. Both bearded and four-parted gentian grew in the neighborhood, as did soapberry shrubs with their translucent red fruit. The natives make a dessert called "Indian ice cream" by whipping soapberries with sugar and water. The fruit is also a bear's delight.

This turnout illustrates a phenomenon I often observe about wildflowers. They rarely stay put for long. They are always changing their place of residence. New plants appear where old ones were and the old ones move on to new locations or disappear. I realize there are many factors involved in this phenomena. The weather, of course, and soil; but the fact that many plants are annuals, their seed carried on the wind, is per-

Milepost 1379
Alaska Highway, B.C.

1 Four-parted Gentian
   Gentiana propingua
2 Thoroughwax
   Bupleurum triradiatum
3 Bearded Gentian
   Gentiana barbata

4 Alpine Meadow Bistort
   Polygonum viviparum
5 Pineapple Weed
   Matricaria matricarioides
6 Soapberry, *Shepherdia canadensis*
7 Pussytoes, *Antennaria sp.*

haps the strongest contributor to their evolution or change of habitat. This is especially noticeable in Alaska where road crews replace the native perennial plants with annual seeds as they upgrade the roads. I am continuously finding new plant combinations, disappointing in some ways, but exciting in others as I return to loved spots such as this one.

LIARD HOT SPRINGS PROVINCIAL PARK
Milepost 447~Highway 97
British Columbia

Undoubtedly this park has to be considered one of the loveliest spots of the 1520-mile Alaska Highway. There is a very special confluence of nature's treasures in this location: wildlife, big and small, more than 200 species of wildflowers, hot springs, and noble woods. The park has been developed with such imagination and insight that it is a favorite stopping place for everyone who passes, whether to bathe, to camp, or just walk to the springs.

The Alpha and Beta pools are as they originally were, secluded in the woods, approached now only by a long boardwalk that protects the fragile ecology of the surroundings. Moose are often seen feeding on the sides of the boardwalk. One year we saw two moose, one on each side of the walk; that evening a cow and her calf appeared in the same location. Rare orchids and delicate brook lobelia bloom in the moist habitat. Tiny fish dart among the water plants growing in the runoff from the pools; birds also bob and swim in the warm shallows. It is an area of precious beauty and serenity. Between the pools in the woods there is a natural hanging garden of exquisite loveliness, best viewed in June and July. On each of our visits to this park in July, we saw completely different plants flowering.

To get a campsite here during the summer, it is best to arrive as early as possible in the morning, as the park fills up very rapidly. Campsites are commodious, private, and attractive because of the towering trees and native shrubs that surround them.

On our last visit every park bench had a sign attached to it warning of bears. In fact for miles on either side of this park we had seen signs saying, "A fed bear is a dead bear." We had scarcely retired for the

1 Baneberry, *Actaea rubra*
2 Marsh Skullcap, *Scutellaria galericulata*
3 Field Mint, *Mentha arvensis*
4 Brook Lobelia, *Lobelia Kalmii*

5 Yellow Monkey-flower, *Mimulus guttatus*
6 Long-leaf Fleabane
   Erigeron lonchophyllus
7 Black Snake-root, *Sanicula marilandica.*

1 Red Twig Dogwood, *Cornus stolonifera*
2 Smooth Aster, *Aster laevis*
3 Sticky False Asphodel
    Tofieldia glutinosa
4 Tundra Rose, *Potentilla fruticosa*

5 Northern Green Bog Orchid
    Platanthera hyperborea
6 High-bush Cranberry, *Viburnum edule*
7 Common Juniper
    Juniperus communis

night when two shots rang out nearby. An unusual noise in a park! In the morning we learned that a camper had forgotten to put his dog food away. A bear came and sat on his table to eat it. The park ranger's shots were to frighten him away. However, the morning found him near the boardwalk alarming the guests. A big bear trap rested in one of the back campsites, reminding us of the proximity of these wild guests. The balance of wildlife and humans is very delicate in this park; utmost care is being taken to protect the interests of both.

Many people fly into and out of Alaska because of time restraints. I always feel so sorry for them as we turn into the Liard Hot Springs Park. I know that they will have missed something very special by not being able to pause at this oasis in the woods. It is an experience never to be forgotten.

Bee on Aster

Alberta, Canada

ALBERTA TRANSPORTATION UTILITIES SITE
West of Whitecourt, Highway 43

HEAD-SMASHED-IN BUFFALO JUMP
Highway 3 at Fort Macleod

WATERTON LAKES NATIONAL PARK
Highway 5 or 17

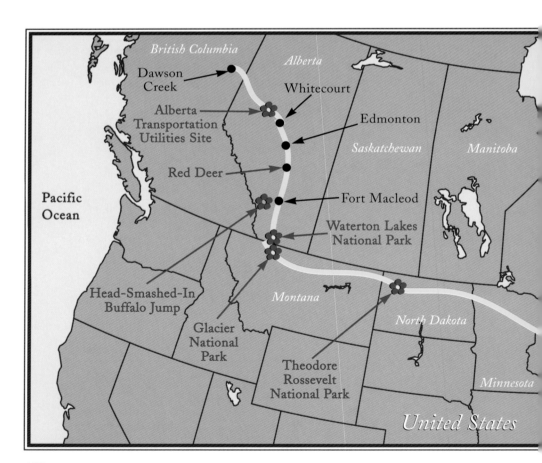

United States

GLACIER NATIONAL PARK
Route 89, Montana

ROOSEVELT NATIONAL PARK, NORTH UNIT
Route 85, North Dakota

SOLDIER LAKE NATIONAL FOREST
Route 28, Michigan

Canada

SAMUEL DE CHAMPLAIN PROVINCIAL PARK
Highway 17, Ontario

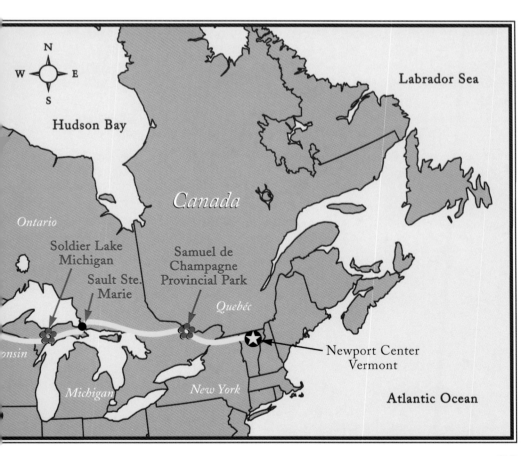

After so many miles of going north and south, into and out of British Columbia, the Yukon, and Alaska, we arrived at Dawson Creek, B.C., the end of the Alaska Highway. Our great Alaskan adventure was over. We now headed east towards Edmonton, Alberta, and home 3000 miles away.

Any disappointment at seeing the close of this part of our trip was short-lived. The landscape took on a whole new appearance—that of the prairies colored with some of the most gorgeous roadside wildflowers imaginable. Paintbrush was especially prevalent and white, pink, and red clover escaped from the nearby cultivated fields.

The small Transportation Utilities campsite is about 248 miles east of Dawson Creek and 120 miles northwest of Edmonton. While primitive, it is clean and offers a small woods trail for campers. It was while on this trail that I came upon the rare green spurred gentian, which I had never seen before, and rediscovered *Achillea sibirica*, a relative of the common yarrow. Sibirica's leaves have a simpler and more deeply serrated appearance. I first became acquainted with this plant in a gravel pit in the Yukon. A wide variety of other wildflowers flourished in this small campsite as well as along the river adjacent to it.

As we moved closer to Edmonton, the flatness of the prairies was no longer relieved by myriad flowers growing along the roadsides. All were now being mowed. A new policy was in place. Travelers are the poorer for this decision.

1 Indian Paintbrush, *Castillega sp.*
2 Yarrow, *Achillea sibirica*
3 Scarlet Paintbrush
   Castillega coccinea

4 Tansy, *Tanacetum vulgare*
5 Spurred Gentian, *Halenia deflexa*
6 Red Clover, *Trifolium pratense*
7 Canada Thistle, *Cirsium arvense*

Ripening Canola Fields in Alberta

HEAD-SMASHED-IN BUFFALO JUMP
Highway 3 at Fort Macleod
Alberta, Canada

South out of Edmonton on Highway 2 one passes through the prairie cities of Calgary and Red Deer. On both sides of the road there are vast fields of ripening wheat and yellowing canola. Grain lies at the heart of this region. Finally Fort Macleod, an early mounted police outpost, is reached, and one turns right for Head-Smashed-In Buffalo Jump. In a few miles a museum appears, a massive structure built into the ridge of the buffalo jump. It commemorates the early Indians of this region, their traditions, their god, Napi, and the buffalo. Buffalo jumps are not uncommon in the West. Herded to a point by the Native peoples the buffalo were then driven over the cliff to their death. This cooperative effort assured the tribes of greater abundance of food and provisions.

The eye-catching name of this park comes from a true story of an Indian brave who wanted to experience the falling of the buffalo more closely. To do this he sequestered himself on a narrow shelf in the cliff behind where the buffalo would fall. He was crushed to death by the downward hurtling animals.

Starting on the long pathway from the east parking area to the museum, one is greeted by the prairie scarlet gaura. This gay flower is best seen in the early morning when it first comes out, for its delicate structures wither under the heat of the prairie sun. The crested wheatgrass, *Agropyron cristatum*, native to the Eurasian Steppes and now growing in the West, intermingles with foxtail, lupine, and yarrow. The purplish awns of the foxtails announce their presence by shimmering in the light, but they also cause irritating distress to grazing cattle. The viper's bugloss, which grows halfway up the path, is most surprising to see in this location. The only other place I have seen this plant is in eastern Canada in the moist gullies lining the roadsides, but I now understand that it grows in scattered places in the West. Unlike many of the plants of this area, which seem withdrawn because of lack of moisture, bugloss grows stoutly and its blue flowers flourish. In contrast, lupine, pussytoe, yarrow, and wild geranium are small, barely flowering. Wild roses bloom by the trail as it goes under the shadow of the great cliff where buffalo were forced to their death in an earlier time.

It is very special to hike along to the top of the jump. The sacredness of the area to the early people seems almost palpable. Some areas are restricted to non-native people. As one strolls out along the cliff, the

1   Bugloss, *Echium vulgare*
2   Yellow Umbrella Plant
     Eriogonum flavum
3   Scarlet Gaura
     Gaura coccinea
4   Small Lupine, *Lupinus pusillus*

5   Crested Wheatgrass
     Agropyron cristatum
6   Scarlet Globemallow
     Sphaeralcea coccinea
7   Prairie-Smoke, *Geum triflorum*
8   Groundsel, *Senecio sp.*

orange of the small scarlet globemallow catches the eye, as does the pea and yellow groundsel. It seems particularly inspiring, as one sees the various wildflowers in this area, to realize that many of the plant varieties have been here for decades—known and used by the Indians for food, medicine, dyes. One sees many Native Indian museums in the West, but the historical significance of this spot, the authenticity of the museum displays, and its location in the vast sweep on the plains, make each visit to Head-Smashed-In a unique experience.

WATERTON-GLACIER INTERNATIONAL PEACE PARK
Waterton Lakes National Park, Highway 5 or 17

There is a region astride the international border in the Rocky mountains of such magnificence that both Canada and the United States established national parks there. Waterton Lakes National Park in southern Alberta and adjoining Glacier National Park in northern Montana share a common cultural heritage, a common geological formation, and the same diversity of plants and animals. Through the efforts of local citizens on both sides of the border, the respective national governments recognized these facts and designated these parks as the first International Peace Park in the world in 1932, an example of what friendship and cooperation can achieve. The special uniqueness of this area was further recognized in 1995, when Waterton-Glacier International Peace Park was designated a World Heritage Site, as being of interest to all humankind and as deserving protection for the benefit of all humanity.

In Waterton Lakes the vast prairie collides with the Canadian Rockies. The unique flow of moisture in this region is such that wildflowers grow in abandon and in incredible variety. Although only about forty miles south of Head-Smashed-In, where all vegetation suffers from great dryness, here the flora flourish with great exuberance. Driving through the prairie grasses filled with paintbrush, tangles of geraniums, death camas, and gallardia, one eventually comes to a mountain valley. The large Crandell Campground stretches along one side of it. At our campsite and in the adjacent fields were mariposa lily, yellow columbine, white thistle, fleabane, northern gentian, ragworts. The Red Rock Canyon trail at the end of the valley is equally flower-filled, especially

very
sticky

1 Wild Bergamot
   Monarda fistulosa
2 Northern Gentian
   Gentiana amarella
3 Common Ragwort
   Senecio aurus

4 Dotted Gayfeather
   Liatrus punctata
5 Gumweed
   Grindelia squarrosa
6 Fleabane sp., *Erigeron sp.*
7 Owlclover, *Orthocarpus tenuifolius*

White Thistle
Cirsium hookeriarum

Alpine Arnica
Arnica alpina

Sticky
Geranium
*Geranium
viscossimum*

Yellow Paintbrush
Castilleja wrightii

Indian Paintbrush
Castilleja sp.

128

Balsam Ragwort
Senecio pauperculus

Wild Gaillardia
Gaillardia aristata

Yellow
Columbine
*Aquilegia
flavescens*

Tall Purple
Fleabane
*Erigeron
peregrinus*

Common Stonecrop
Sedum lanceolatum

Orange
Hawkweed
*Hieracium
aurantiacum*

when the trail bursts into sunlight at the falls. A small hawkweed, orange in color and found in New England, was discovered among the many unfamiliar plants. Some of my flowers come from our drive to Cameron Lake on the Akamina Parkway. This alpine lake, whose far side lies in Glacier National Park, is like a precious blue gem set in the mountains.

Waterton Lakes National Park will always be the highlight in my traveling with wildflowers. The coincidence of sunshine, timing, temperature, and abundant moisture was so ideal, that never before, nor since, have I seen such a variety of glorious wildflowers.

WATERTON-GLACIER INTERNATIONAL PEACE PARK
Glacier National Park, Route 89, Montana, U.S.A.

As we leave Waterton Lake on Route 17, the landscape becomes dominated by the great Chief Mountain on the northern edge of Glacier National Park. This monolith rises out of the earth in much the same way that Denali Mountain does in Alaska, seeming to gather all the earth to it as it grows upward. The great reverence that the Native peoples have for this mountain is easily understood; its solitary majesty is inspiring.

A few miles south of the U. S. border one is greeted by the road leading into Many Glaciers, the first campground of several in the park. Tucked up against the Rockies, it provides early July visitors with a stunning show of flowering bear grass. This torch-like plant grows in every sunlit space among the alpine spruce and fir trees around the campsites and trails. Its hundreds of dainty, small cream-white flowers—each on a white shaft springing from a single stalk out of a green, grass-like base—make it one of the most glorious flowers seen anywhere. Its makes every spot in which it grows glow. Local people informed us that 1996 was a year of extraordinary flowering, such as occurs only every six or seven years.

Our next stop was St. Mary's Campground just inside the Visitors' Center of the park. The view of Glacier's great peaked mountains from this location, and everything else about the park, is worth the thousands of miles of driving required to get here. Comprising over a

Glacier National Park

1 Common Harebell
   Campanula rotundifolia
2 Blanket Flower, *Gaillardia aristata*
3 Wild Prairie Rose, *Rosa arkansana*
4 Wild Onion, *Allium sp.*

5 Decumbent Goldenrod
   Solidago decumbens
6 Field Bindweed
   Convolvulus arvensis
7 Knapweed, *Centaurea maculosa*

million acres, it is about eight times larger than its sister park, Waterton. Although split in half by the continental divide, Glacier is united by the Road to the Sun. It connects Lake St. Mary on the eastern side of the divide with the larger Lake McDonald on the western side. A marvel of engineering skill, the road has recently been closed to all vehicles over twenty-one feet. Special park minibuses now navigate the narrow curves, which were becoming too dangerous for the ever longer motor homes and camping trailers.

John Muir once wrote of Glacier National Park, "Give a month at least to this precious reserve. The time will not be taken from the sum of your life. Instead of shortening, it will indefinitely lengthen it and make you truly immortal." Our three visits scarcely encompassed a week in total, but there is much we will never forget: our hike to Hidden Lake from Logan Pass through the many hues of Indian paintbrush, the glorious beauty of McDonald Lake in the morning stillness of another visit, driving the whole distance around the park in order to see the great animal salt lick in the south, and a hundred other treasured memories. This park is justly designated a World Heritage Site.

The Saga of the Western Salsify
or
How to Paint Flowers While Your Husband Drives

About two months and about 13,500 miles before we reached Glacier National Park, we were in Cache Creek, British Columbia, just about to start the Alaskan part of our adventure. My husband was taking a last minute video of Cache Creek Campground when suddenly I saw a yellow star blooming. The flower, exquisite in the morning sunshine, was unknown to me.

Pushing to be off, my driver told me there was no time to paint. With some trepidation I cut the flower, put it in water, and eagerly awaited our first stop. But alas, when we finally stopped, the star was closed, never to open again.

In the Fraser Valley, many miles later, we stopped for a few photographs. I unexpectedly found another star flower. This time I was told that the road was too narrow for us to stay any longer. Again I picked the flower and put it in water. What I did not know at that time was that this flower blooms only in sunshine. It too was closed when we finally stopped. I painted what I could: the stem and leaves.

Although I continued to look for the now-identified western salsify, I was not to catch another glimpse of it as we traveled into and out of Alaska. But there is justice for wildflower painters! And it came in Glacier National Park.

We were in St. Mary's Campground. My husband had become like a horse running for the home barn 2500 miles away. I was told we could have only an overnight in Glacier. Morning brought a change of thought. He said we could drive to Logan Pass on the Road to the Sun and hike a little, provided we could find a parking space. Halfway up we were halted by the summer road crew. Imagine being forced to stop for fifteen minutes before the most glorious mountain view any artist could ever wish to sketch. However, there was to be no hiking for us that day. We could not find an inch of available parking space, much less the twenty-eight feet we needed.

Winding back down the pass road, the same road crew stopped us again. This time I said I was going to get out and look around at the wildflowers. "No, no I won't wait for you," was the reply. I got out anyway. On returning to the motor home, I saw a western salsify right by the door—blooming! I picked it, went inside, and painted it. Thirty-five minutes later we were at last allowed to move and I had captured my flower.

Western Salsify

THEODORE ROOSEVELT NATIONAL PARK
North Unit
Route 85, North Dakota

Our recent discovery of the North Unit of this great park has been an experience of unparalleled delight. Unlike the South Unit, where one looks out and down upon the badlands, here one drives through the great eroded shapes. It is easily approached by Route 85 connecting the great northern highways 2 and 94 traversing the American West.

A wonderfully shaded campground down by the Missouri River in the park called Squaw Creek comes as a welcome relief in this generally arid region. Starting on the Scenic Drive at the Visitors' Center, the badlands tower above, the fine winding road gradually rises above the eroded shapes to the high prairie grasslands plateau. As we rounded the last bend, we saw a herd of about a hundred buffalo in the flower-filled fields. It is a sight that few are privileged to see today. The fifteen-mile road ends a few miles further at Sperati Point. Here one is greeted with a panoramic view of the badlands with the Little Missouri River flowing like a thread of light far below.

Spring is an extraordinary time in the North Unit. The landscape is suffused with the pale yellow of sweet clover lying in great drifts wherever the land is flat enough to permit its growth. Because of the nature of the road, one sometimes sees the clover up close, other times as a subtle haze in the distance. For miles it glorifies the landscape. Occasionally the mild low white Seneca root is interspersed with it.

Sagebrush dots the dry badland. This tough blue-gray shrub is at home on all lands of the arid west. On the self-guiding Caprock-Coulee trail one learns that this park has three varieties of sagebrush. In the shadows of the eroded forms, many different flowers flourish—thistles, cactus, silver buffaloberry, pentstemons. This trail provides an in-depth explanation of the badlands' formations and is well worth taking.

The North Unit of the park is equally enjoyable in August when the purple of the prairie coneflowers fill the grasses with color, and the stiff goldenrods with their brilliant cadmium yellow flowers shout their presence. My flower painting is from this period.

It was while on our August visit on the high prairie that a great bull buffalo blocked the road, matching his might against modern vehicles. Traffic stopped and everyone stood around cautiously taking pictures, not only of the great bull, but of the homely calves, cows, and other bulls feeding nearby. Suddenly a Ford Explorer burst upon the scene and drove right up to the massive bull. When he did not move, the driver

1

2

rough like
sandpaper

3

5

4

6

coarse
hairy

7

1 Evening Star, *Mentzelia decapetala*
2 Rough Sunflower
   Helianthus rigidus
3 Rigid Goldenrod, *Solidago rigida*
4 Purple Prairie-Clover
   Dalea purpurea

5 Prairie Coneflower
   Ratibida columnifera
6 Silver Buffaloberry
   Sherpherdia argentea
7 Purple Coneflower
   Echinacea angustifolia

blew his horn impatiently. The buffalo ignored him. The driver blew his horn again. The bull continued to stand immobile. Finally the driver jerked his car around and sped off. In this spot, for at least a moment, this great animal had dominion over his world again. The bull and the herd eventually moved on and everyone resumed their driving.

One cannot come in contact with the badlands' infinite shapes, the layering of colors, the eons of time they represent, or the wildlife living in their borders without being touched with wonder. The badlands are truly one of nature's masterpieces.

SOLDIER LAKE NATIONAL FOREST
Route 28, Michigan

The national forests in Michigan provide camping opportunities at all levels from primitive to developed. Soldier Lake, in the latter category, offers opportunities to swim, fish, hike, and bike, and is one of the parks where an abundance of wildflowers can be easily discovered. Mowing, the scourge of flower lovers, is at a minimum in this park. Soldier Lake has the added attraction of never being crowded.
Lining the roads is the sweet fern or wild tea. The leaves of this fern-like perennial bush were a tea substitute for the early colonists. A wealth of dwarf blueberry and wintergreen cover the ground. Leatherleaf abounds around the lake and is even more noticeable if one takes the dirt road to the adjacent pond. Along the road to the beach one can see evening primrose, aster, yarrow, pearly everlasting, and on the edges of the more heavily wooded areas, green orchid. The seeker of wildflowers could easily pass a day studying the extensive variety of plants found in this area.

Soldier Lake combines so many different elements that make camping a delight, one is surprised it is not more utilized. We found it a most pleasing stopping place when going either east or west.

1. Low Blueberry, *Vaccinium vacillans*
2. Bullrush, *Scripus acutus*
3. Haircap Moss
   Polytrichum juniperinum
4. Blue Vervain, *Verbena hastata*
5. Evening Primrose
   Oenothera biennis
6. Smooth Aster
   Aster laevis
7. Sweet Fern, *Myrica aspenifolia*
8. Leatherleaf,
   Chamaedaphne calyculata
9. Wintergreen
   Gaultheria procumbens

SAMUEL DE CHAMPLAIN PROVINCIAL PARK
15 miles west of Mattawa, Ontario, Highway 17

If one wishes the quickest and shortest route back to New England after leaving Soldier Lake National Forest Campground in Michigan, enter Canada at nearby Sault Ste. Marie and take Highway 17 east. It is not the most scenic route nor the best road, but one will discover amazing Sudbury, an international hub for business and a moonscape that pollution from the nickel mines and smelters created. It was to this area that the first astronauts came to train. It is also on this road that one finds the excellent Samuel de Champlain Provincial Park.

Voyageur: A man employed by the fur companies to carry goods and people to and from the trading posts on the lakes and rivers of Canada starting in the 1700s. There were two types of "voyageurs," the "Hivernants" who wintered at the Northwest trading posts, and the "Pork Eaters" who paddled the local Montreal run.

This is just one of the many interesting facts that can be learned at the superb museum in this park, where one finds a replica of a 36-Foot birch bark canoe, used at the time Samuel de Champlain was making his westward explorations in the early 1600s. These large canoes carried up to three tons of provisions and required paddlers of enormous strength. Here is found information about the two great fur companies of the north—Hudson's Bay and North West—who fought each other for fur rights until they merged in 1820. One learns about the Nipissings, the Indians of the woodlands, who inhabited this region. Information is presented in such a fresh and visual way that it pleases all who enter the museum, especially the young people.

Samuel de Champlain Park is large and varied. There is the splendid Bagwa beach for swimming, good interior roads, and trails for biking and hiking. One can camp in the open or in the cool of great woods.

The Wabashkiki trail takes one into a wet environs with a loop up onto a forested island, an hour walk. (Wabashkiki means marsh in Ojibway.) As one walks on the floating boardwalk in late August, one can see most of the flowers pictured in the painting. The range of flowers in bloom is surprising. Normally some of the varieties would have gone by, but the pickerel weed still share the water with the exquisite white pond lily. Great colonies of orange touch-me-not range over much of the low foliage; the bulrush are the highest ever seen, well over six feet. Cardinal

Samuel De Champlain Provincial Park

very
hairy

1 Bulrush, *Scirpus acutus*
2 Touch-me-not, *Impatiens capensis*
3 Bugleweed, *Lycopus virginicus*
4 Pickerel Weed, *Pontedaria cordata*

5 Viper's Bugloss, *Echium vulgare*
6 Fragrant Water-lily
   Nymphaea odorata
7 Cardinal Flower, *Lobelia cardinalis*

flower, preferring different soil, grow along the banks of the Amable du Fond River, which flows through the park. The viper's bugloss is from the parking area by the museum. There is much more to be explored and experienced in this park, if one has the time—more trails, walks with the park naturalist, boating, and fishing.

This park always marks the end of my painting while traveling. The thought of home is too strong for dallying. Brushes and paper and books are put away as we race along the last 500 miles of the return trip.

Chocolate
Geum

All flowers were painted from the actual flower with the exception of deer cabbage. Unfortunately I thought it was buckbean and did not attend to its flower soon enough.

Landscapes were sandwiched in when moments permitted. Most had to be done quickly. Perfection was never an option. I was often sketching as we drove—the view of my subject changing as we moved by it!

I wish everyone could have the wonderful experiences we have had while traveling.